The
illustra-
tion on the
cover shows the
figurehead of the "King
Philip" — one of the clippers
mentioned in this brochure. To the
sailors of days gone by the figurehead typified
the presiding genius of the ship, and they prophe-
sied all sorts of dire things when shipowners began to skimp
on their outlays for figureheads. The figurehead
was the heritage of early man's supersti-
tions and the custom of having one
adorn the bow of the ship traces
back to the days when an-
cient craft were adorned
with figures of
gods and god-
desses.

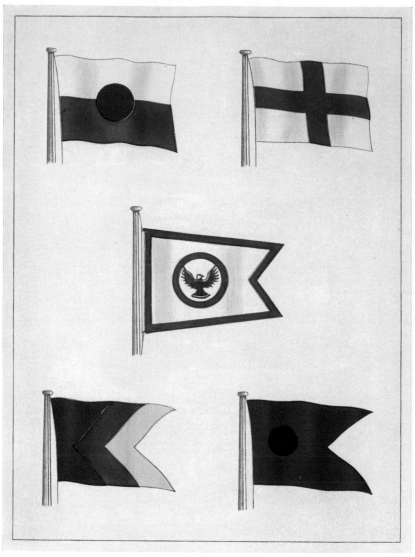

From "Some Famous Sailing Ships and Their Builder Donald McKay"
By Richard C. McKay

HOUSE FLAGS CARRIED BY DONALD McKAY'S CLIPPERS

MESSRS. SAMPSON & TAPPAN,
Boston

GEORGE B. UPTON
Boston

DONALD McKAY
Boston

GRINNELL, MINTURN & CO.
New York
(*California Line*)

JAMES BAINES & CO.
Liverpool, England
(*Australian Black Ball Line*)

OTHER YANKEE
Ship Sailing Cards

Presenting more reproductions
of the colorful cards
announcing ship sailings
to California and other Pacific ports
in the days when the
California Gold Rush
led to the development of
fast sailing clippers
and able and courageous men
to sail them

By
ALLAN FORBES
and
RALPH M. EASTMAN

Issued by the
STATE STREET TRUST COMPANY
BOSTON, MASSACHUSETTS

Ye bloods of the present day,
To you I have nothing to say,
Except ye are able,
To splice a chain cable,
And get a sheer hulk under way.
BASIL LUBBOCK

FOREWORD

OUR 1948 BROCHURE on this subject seemed to meet with such a flattering reception that we thought another volume might be warranted and would prove acceptable.

This time we have tried not only to select particularly attractive cards but also those which advertised clippers with somewhat unusual, and many times curious, names. Many of these vessels, it will be seen, had interesting histories, which warrant their inclusion in this volume. It will be noted also that practically all of them advertised sailings to San Francisco, and this seems timely and appropriate because 1949 is the hundredth anniversary of the great California gold rush which brought that State to the attention of the whole civilized world and led to its development into one of the most important in the Union. While many of these cards announced sailings from New York, we have been able to maintain our leaning toward items of New England interest because so many of these vessels were either built in this section of the country or were commanded by skippers who hailed from the various New England States, particularly Massachusetts, and often from Cape Cod.

Gold was first discovered at Sutter's Mill, Coloma, California, on January 24, 1848 but it was not till many months later that the news of it percolated across the nation and the real rush to the Golden State got underway. The era of the fabulous '49ers has always held a romantic interest for the people of this country and it is a pleasure to include in this brochure bits of information which show the important role the ship captains and seamen, as well as the clippers built in New England, played in transporting adventurers and cargoes to San Francisco during that period. Great impetus was given by the gold rush to the building of swift vessels of transport and this was responsible for the launching of 160 clippers within 4 years. It is said that during the year before the discovery of the first

v

nugget in California only two ships from Atlantic ports had visited San Francisco Bay. In the year and a half that followed more than 700 vessels sailed into that magnificent harbor, bringing around 100,000 persons who had need of food, clothing, and working tools, which meant the prices of such things went sky-high and made their transportation in most cases a fabulously profitable business. As a matter of fact, it was not unusual for a clipper to pay for herself on a single round-trip voyage, and many times with considerable profit besides. Many fortunes were made by suppliers who did not have to go to the trouble of seeking the more glamorous gold. Shoes at one time sold for $75 a pair, which gives an idea as to costs.

In hundreds of cases, such was the effect of the craze for gold on the minds of its seekers that vessels on arriving at San Francisco were run aground and abandoned by their passengers and crews. There were 500 deserted ships in the harbor by July of 1850, according to the Encyclopædia Britannica. Of the 80,000 men reaching the West Coast in 1849, it is estimated that 40,000 went by sea. Hordes of gold seekers, instead of going by ship around the Horn, took the route across the Isthmus of Panama, from Chagres to Panama, by boat and mule, if fortunate enough to be able to hire, or buy, one of the animals. Many died of cholera or other diseases or mishaps. Those who got through endured terrible hardships on the way, especially those who covered much of the distance on foot, carrying all their impedimenta. It was during this period that Chagres, a small village of the Republic of Panama, on the Atlantic coast, at the mouth of the Chagres River, reached its greatest importance.

That this gold rush had a lasting impact on the language and literature of our times is indicated by the fact that one definition of the word "argonaut" in many present-day dictionaries is "One of those who went to California in search of gold shortly after its discovery there in 1848." Also, an interesting book by Octavius Thorndike Howe is entitled "Argonauts of '49."

ACKNOWLEDGMENTS

We wish particularly to express appreciation to the following persons for the help given us in the preparation of this volume: Clarence S. Brigham of the American Antiquarian Society, Worcester, Lawrence W. Jenkins of the Peabody Museum of Salem, Edward H. Redstone of the Boston Public Library, and his staff, as well as James L. Bruce of the Bostonian Society, all of whom were most gracious throughout the past year in furnishing us with reference books or information without which we could not have assembled the material presented herein.

Others to whom we are indebted for assistance are: Roger Amory, U. E. Baughman, Admiral E. L. Cochrane, Charles Brewer, Dexter H. Chamberlain, Allan P. Chase, Claude F. Clement, William E. Crosby, Francis A. Crowley, John E. Cullinan, Archibald J. Dalzell, Benjamin Dill, William C. Edwards, Mrs. Emma Gray Francis, G. Peabody Gardner, Mrs. Helen S. Giffen, Mark W. Hennessey, Miss Alice G. Higgins, August Hirschbaum, Kenneth Howes, James M. Hunnewell, Miss Frances L. Hyland, Miss Helena Mills John, Mrs. Margaret Joyce, T. Edward Kellar, Carl T. Keller, Miss Lucrezia Kemper, Paul E. Landry, Hon. Henry Cabot Lodge, Jr., Francis B. Lothrop, Richard C. McKay, Richard M. Oddie, Russell G, Palmer, Miss Josepha M. Perry, Herbert Gleason Porter, Gorham Pulsifer, Harry C. Rodd, W. L. Skelton, Stephen J. Spingarn, George H. Thacher, L. E. Townsend, Walter F. Trundy, Harry C. Webber, Miss Helen J. Williamsen, also the following organizations — California Historical Society, Cape Ann Scientific, Literary & Historical Association, Cohasset Historical Society, Thomas Crane Public Library, Harvard University Graduate School of Business Administration, Hyannis Public Library Association, The Library of Congress, Maine Historical Society, Medford Historical Society and Rhode Island Historical Society.

We also desire to give public recognition to the devoted service of Miss Katherine G. Rogers and Miss Margaret M. Burke in typing the manuscript and the considerable volume of correspondence necessary in the preparation of this brochure.

Those who are interested in delving further into the subject of clipper ships will find, as we did, the following books especially worthy of perusal:

"American Clipper Ships" by Octavius T. Howe, M.D. and Frederick C. Matthews

"Argonauts of '49" by Octavius T. Howe, M.D.

"The Clipper Ship Era" by Captain Arthur H. Clark

"Greyhounds of the Sea" by Carl C. Cutler

★　　　★　　　★

Courtesy L. W. Jenkins, Salem

A piece of crockery from a set used on one of the packets in the fleet of the important firm of Train & Company of Boston.

The original of this illustration, with at least one other item from the set, is on exhibition in the Peabody Museum, Salem.

*I*T has been our custom to issue from time to time publications designed to prove enjoyable and of historical value to our friends. We trust that this thirty-third brochure will succeed in fulfilling this desire.

We also hope that the impression received will be so favorable that the reader will feel that our publications typify the institution which issues them and that the high standard maintained in their form and material is characteristic of the banking and trust service we render.

We shall be very happy if the pleasure derived from our brochures induces our friends to think favorably of the State Street Trust Company when the occasion arises for opening a new bank account, financing the purchase of an automobile or household appliances, or renting a safe deposit box at any of our four offices. We also have storage facilities for silverware and other bulky valuables at our Main and Massachusetts Avenue offices.

It may be that some of our readers are not aware of the fact that our Trust Department is qualified by experience to serve effectively as Agent in the handling of investments, as Trustee of Living Trusts, Pension and Profit Sharing Plans, Life Insurance Trusts, as Executor and Trustee under wills and in any other recognized trust capacity.

It will be a pleasure to us to furnish to those interested detailed information in regard to any of the various services which we render.

ALLAN FORBES,
President, State Street Trust Company

Boston, 1949

THE INDEPENDENT GOLD HUNTER ON HIS WAY TO CALIFORNIA

*From a rare hand-colored lithograph by N. Currier
in the collection of the State Street Trust Company*

x

TABLE OF CONTENTS

PAGE

House Flags Carried by Donald McKay's Clippers . . ii
The Independent Gold Hunter on His Way to California . x
The Way They Go to California xii
Bengal 1– 3
Black Hawk 4– 6
Bostonian 7– 8
Boston Light 9– 11
Bunker Hill 12– 13
Contest 14– 16
Cremorne 17– 18
Derby 19– 20
Don Quixote 21– 23
Eagle Wing 24– 25
Emerald Isle 26– 27
Empress of the Seas 28– 29
Franklin 30– 32
Gamecock 32– 35
Garibaldi 35– 37
George Peabody 38– 42
Grace Darling 43– 44
Great Republic 45   47
Hornet 48– 52
Huguenot 53– 54
John Gilpin 55– 57
King Philip 58– 60
Masonic 61– 62
Neptune's Favorite 63– 64
Ocean Express 65– 66
Onward 67– 71
Osborn Howes 72– 74
Sancho Panza 74– 76
Seaman's Bride 77– 78
Spitfire 79– 81
Syren 82– 83
Thatcher Magoun 84– 86
Westward Ho 87   95
William Tell 96– 97
Wizard 98–100
Visual Telegraphs 101–103
The Parker House of San Francisco 104
California Gold Centennial Postage Stamp 105–106

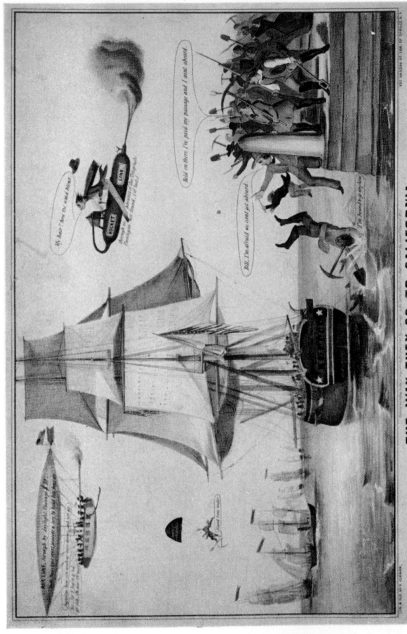

THE WAY THEY GO TO CALIFORNIA.

From the collection of the State Street Trust Company

The prophesies made in 1849 by N. Currier, the publisher of this picture, are astonishing, showing a steamer; an air liner; a passenger, with pick and shovel, landing by parachute; and a rocket plane. This unusual print was colored by Mrs. Doris McGuiggan, daughter of Chester H. Phillips of The Old Picture Store, Boston.

xii

OTHER YANKEE
Ship Sailing Cards

★　　　★　　　★

BENGAL

As THIS CHAPTER is being written a tiger, described by the newspapers as from Bengal, escaped from a zoo in a suburb of Boston, mauling its keeper and causing the visitors to make a hasty exit. A shot ended its existence.

Since the word "Bengal," to most people, is practically synonymous with the famous tigers, we will digress for a few moments and describe a few points about this beautiful but dreaded animal. The officers of the Trust Company are not familiar with the tiger(!) but a few authorities on the subject have been consulted.

Among some natives, according to a big game hunter, it is believed that those versed in occult arts can transform themselves into tigers when desired and thereafter be invulnerable. There is also a creed in parts of India that the spirits of those men who have been killed by tigers place themselves on the animal's head and warn it against danger. Another legend concerns a mischievous boy who was flogged by his schoolmaster with the result that he was transformed into a tiger and this is the reason why tigers are striped. Some natives contend that the stripes were formed by nature to harmonize with the light streaks and shades of the Indian jungle. There is also a belief that the fat of a tiger rubbed on a painful part of a person's body brings instant relief, while others think the whiskers and teeth of the tiger act as charms, thereby making the wearer immune against attack.

Some tigers are very clever, and according to James Inglis in his "Reminiscences on the Nepal Frontier," he once saw a tiger hide from his attacker beneath the water except for its eyes, ears

ANOTHER MAGNIFICENT A 1 CLIPPER SHIP !!

Large Engagements and Quick Dispatch !!

Merchants' Express Line of Clipper Ships
FOR SAN FRANCISCO !

THE SPLENDID A 1 CLIPPER SHIP

BENGAL

MELVILLE, Commander,

Will receive the balance of her cargo at Pier 13 East River. This splendid Clipper is owned and fitted out by the owners of the celebrated Clippers CYCLONE and MAMELUKE, and compares favorably with those vessels. She was built SPECIALLY for the CHINA TRADE and is splendidly ventilated. She comes to the berth with nearly ONE-HALF OF HER CARGO ACTUALLY ON BOARD, and, consequently, will fill up VERY QUICKLY.

RANDOLPH M. COOLEY & CO., 88 Wall St.,

Ag'ts in San Francisco, Messrs. DE WITT, KITTLE & CO. (TONTINE BUILDING.)

Courtesy of American Antiquarian Society, Worcester, Mass.

and nose. Still a more curious tale concerning them. Often they would swim from island to island but if there was a tide they would be drowned in the sacred Ganges. Inglis claims to have seen them often dip their tails into the stream to find out which way the tide was flowing and if the tide was in their favor they would venture in, otherwise they would remain on land.

A curious fact is that the female man-eating tigers are more dangerous than the male. Inglis states that sometimes whole villages have been depopulated which once were flourishing hamlets. Whole herds have been destroyed, but in due time the tiger learned that it is much easier to kill a human being than a cow and hence the danger confronting the hunter. Blanford writing of Ceylon and Burma states that in Lower Burma between 1860 and 1866, 4,218 persons were killed by these animals.

The name Bengal may, however, have been selected for this clipper to compare the fighting qualities of the tiger with a vessel which was to battle so many dangerous elements. It is highly improbable that she was named for Bengal, one of the provinces of Hindustan, as its only harbor is very difficult for shipping, being menaced by many shoals. Another version of the use of such a curious name for this craft, which the card states was built for the China trade, may be accounted for by the fact that a great deal of the tea brought to this country was grown in Bengal. Another important product of that country is tobacco, a large portion of which is exported to Burma where much of it goes into the extra long, white Burma cheroots made famous by Kipling in his "On the Road to Mandalay" by his reference to the Burma girl in the well known words of the British soldier.

The "Bengal" was built at Medford, Mass., in 1840 by Waterman & Ewell for owners Henry Oxnard, Abbott Lawrence, Wm. and James A. Appleton of Boston. She met an untimely end in 1853 when she had to be beached on St. Michael's, Azores, on a trip from Cadiz to Beverly loaded with salt.

NO DELAY IN LOADING.

SUTTON & CO'S DISPATCH LINE FOR

SAN FRANCISCO

CLIPPER OF SATURDAY, 1st DEC.

Sailing Regularly as Advertised.

The Magnificent A 1 First Class New York Built Clipper Ship

BLACK HAWK

BOWERS, Master,

Is receiving her Cargo at PIER 28, EAST RIVER.

The BLACK HAWK *is the only New York built Clipper up*, and favorably known to Shippers as a first-class conveyance, in every respect. "Having the most of her Cargo engaged, she will have our *usual prompt dispatch.*"

SUTTON & CO., 58 SOUTH ST., Cor. Wall.

Special Notice.—Shippers wishing to avoid all delay in loading will bear in mind that the promptness and dispatch of this line is unequaled by any other from New York to San Francisco.

ISAAC J. OLIVER, PRINTER, 32 BEEKMAN,

BLACK HAWK

THE PICTURE used to illustrate the card advertising the sailing of this clipper obviously is supposed to portray that famous American Indian warrior, Black Sparrow Hawk, whose name, by custom, has been contracted to "Black Hawk."

He fought hard for his people in opposing the encroachments of the white man and met with much cruel and shameful treatment until his capture in 1832. He was then confined for a short time at Fortress Monroe, Virginia, after which he was taken by the Government through the principal eastern cities. While arriving at New York from Philadelphia by boat, Black Hawk and his fellow warriors who accompanied him witnessed the balloon ascent of the aeronaut Durant from Castle Garden, which filled the Indians with amazement. This was the most outstanding event of their experiences on their tour. In Baltimore they attended for the first time the theatre and, also, a circus. The latter pleased them more than the former because they understood horsemanship and greatly enjoyed the riding exhibitions — especially seeing the women ride side-saddle. When released from captivity, Black Hawk settled on the Sauk and Fox reservation on the Des Moines River in Iowa, where he died on October 3, 1838. He was a daring chieftain who led his people as best he could in a hopeless struggle.

A statue by Larado Taft was erected to his memory on a high bluff on the Rock River near Oregon, Illinois. This site was chosen as Black Hawk was born in an Indian village on the banks of that river. In 1832 Abraham Lincoln, at the age of 23, enlisted in the so-called "Black Hawk War" and was elected Captain of a company by his friends. He was engaged in no active fighting with the enemy, however; therefore none of the cruelties perpetrated against them can mar his memory. As a matter of fact, it is said that on one occasion he saved from his own men a poor old friendly Indian who came to them with a letter of credentials. The men claimed it was a forgery and were about to hang the poor redskin as a spy when Lincoln appeared on the scene and forced his rather undisciplined company to release their prey.

As an indication that the fierce attitude toward Black Hawk had subsided rapidly in the years following the war, there were two vessels built by 1857 which were given his name. One of these was the work of William H. Webb of New York who built three packet ships in his father's shipyard on the East River, between 5th and 7th Streets, before he was 25. He is said to have launched a greater aggregate tonnage than any other builder and constructed the first steamer to enter the Golden Gate. He was also the founder of the Webb Institute of Naval Architecture in New York City. For the information about Webb we are indebted to "The Lookout," the monthly publication of the Seamen's Church Institute of New York which celebrated its centennial in 1944.

The "Black Hawk" made twenty passages around Cape Horn to San Francisco between 1857 and 1880 — two of which were from Liverpool and eighteen from New York. Her fastest voyage from this latter port to San Francisco was 107 days in 1861. She made one return from San Francisco to New York in 95 days and one to Boston in 97 days.

Her original owners were Bucklin & Crane of New York who sold her in the middle '60s to George Howes & Co. of New York and San Francisco. When the latter firm retired from business around 1880, the "Black Hawk" was sold and operated principally between New York and ports in Germany under the ownership of a German firm. Her name does not appear in shipping registers after 1888. While under the American flag, her commanders were Captains B. P. Bowers, Seth Doane (each for about five years), Hallett, Howland, and Milton B. Crowell, the last four being familiar old Cape Cod names.

Courtesy of Peabody Museum, Salem, Mass.

BOSTONIAN

As MIGHT be guessed from her name, this "elegant first class clipper ship" was built in the environs of Boston for Bostonians. It was D. D. Kelley of East Boston who produced her in 1854 for George Callander & Co., commission merchants, of 43 Central Wharf, Boston. She was sold to New York in November of 1860. On January 2nd, 1861, she was wrecked near Guernsey while bound from New York to London.

It will be noticed that this card, like the majority of those used during the period covered by our brochures on this subject, fails to give the year of the sailing and many do not even give the date, which adds to the difficulty of successful research on the history of these vessels. The active house of William T. Coleman & Co. apparently maintained an office of their own in San Francisco, instead of using local agents in that city as was the general custom.

Daniel D. Kelley, shipwright and calker, commenced building around 1848 and also did a lot of repair work. At various times he was located at Kelly's Wharf and Maverick Wharf off Sumner Street in East Boston. Among the vessels he built was the pilot boat "Fanny" which made a passage from Boston to San Francisco in 107 days, which, for a craft only 71 feet long, was an outstanding accomplishment of the times.

Smallest, Sharpest and Fastest

CLIPPER LOADING.

101 DAYS TO SAN FRANCISCO

Clipper of TUESDAY, April 30th.

The Celebrated A 1 Extreme Clipper Ship

BOSTON LIGHT

HOLWAY, Commander,

Is taking in the last of her Cargo at Pier 9 East River.

This beautiful vessel carries but 1,600 Tons of cargo, and makes extreme clipper time, as above record proves. She insures A 1 Extra, and will have immediate dispatch. For balance of Freight, apply to

RANDOLPH M. COOLEY, 118 Water St., cor. Wall,

Tontine Building.

Agents in San Francisco, Messrs. DE WITT, KITTLE & CO.

Courtesy of American Antiquarien Society

BOSTON LIGHT

IT ALMOST goes without saying that this clipper was built in Boston (by E. & H. O. Briggs) for Boston owners, James Huckins & Sons, whose address at that time was 35 Commercial Wharf. According to Captain Arthur H. Clark, James Huckins was a jolly, kind-hearted gentleman whom everybody liked. His house flag was a white field, swallowtail, with a blue star in the centre, and when he took his two sons into partnership he placed two exceedingly small blue stars in the upper and lower luff of the flag, as he remarked, "to represent their interest in the business."

The Briggs brothers mentioned above as builders of this fast clipper whose record shows that she made the trip from Boston to San Francisco in 102 days, were grandsons of the North River builder James Briggs. In 1773 he built at Scituate the "Columbia" of Boston, which was the first vessel to circumnavigate the globe and was the discoverer of the great river in Oregon which bears her name.

Boston ownership of the "Boston Light" was continued when she was purchased by Henry Hastings of this city, who did business at 50 India Street. He also owned the clippers "Midnight" and "Noonday." In 1863 the "Boston Light" went to owners in India.

It is interesting to note that, according to Captain Clark referred to above, an outstanding authority on clipper ships, while a large number of sailing ships were built for the California trade after the close of the Civil War, it is a notable fact that only two of these vessels made the passage from an Atlantic port to San Francisco in less than 100 days. The two exceptions were the "Seminole" built by Maxson & Fish of Mystic, Connecticut, and the "Glory of the Seas" built by Donald McKay — both New England builders.

Captain Callaghan commanded the "Boston Light" on her maiden trip from Boston to San Francisco, then to Sydney, New South Wales, and on to China, arriving at New York on her return journey on March 25, 1856, after an absence of approximately fifteen months. Under Captain Elkanah Crowell, originally of West Yarmouth, Cape Cod, Mass., and later of Hyannis, she sailed from New York to Melbourne, Australia, then to San Francisco via Hong Kong. She made another trip to Hong Kong before heading back to New York after stopping at Calcutta, India. While in Hong Kong, three years out from the home port, Captain Crowell had such a severe illness that his life was despaired of. After his recovery, his wife, Susan, would never let him sail without her as long as he followed the sea, which meant that she suffered many vicissitudes on account of this decision, but she never faltered.

Captain Holway was in command on the next voyage of the "Boston Light" and ran into heavy gales which did much damage to the ship and injured several men. Captain Sturgis Crowell, brother of Elkanah, assumed command and took this Boston clipper to San Francisco. He, too, ran into more violent gales and had a very uncomfortable time. The figurehead was washed away and, because the rudderhead was carried away, for eight days there was no control whatever over her. After deciding to jettison 100 tons of cargo to lighten the ship to get at the steering gear, they at last got her under control. During the voyage the mate was stabbed by one of the crew and died of his wounds. It was, altogether, a miserable voyage. Some years later, after a run to Bombay she was sold and renamed the "Tulga."

BUNKER HILL

THIS EXTREME CLIPPER was built by James O. Curtis at Medford in 1857 for Curtis and James Lee, Jr. of Boston. Lee is listed in the Boston directory of that year as a partner of James Lee & Co., commission merchants, 9 and 10 India Wharf. In 1863 she was purchased by J. L. Gardner, whose office was at 22 Congress Street, Boston, and home at 7 Beacon Street, at that time. John Lowell Gardner (1804-1883), according to "Famous Families of Massachusetts" by Mary Caroline Crawford, published in 1930 by Little, Brown & Company, Boston, was one of the last of the great East India merchants of New England. He also did considerable trade with Russia. It was said of him, because he was so uniformly successful in his business ventures, that "if you had started him at the foot of State Street with nothing on, by the time he had reached the Old State House he would have a new suit of clothes, spats, cane, a tall hat, and money in his pocket." Isabella Stewart Gardner, the wife of his namesake son, later became a conspicuous member of Boston society and left her home "Fenway Court," commonly known as "Mrs. Jack Gardner's Palace," as a museum and one of the showplaces of present-day Boston.

We were unable to find further information about the "Bunker Hill" except that after being severely damaged by fire at Manila in February of 1875 she was sold to Spanish owners who changed her name to "Elcano."

It was the custom in Medford during the heyday of her shipbuilding industry to dismiss the children from school on the gala days of ship launchings; so, no doubt, the youngsters were all in favor of more and better business for the bustling shipyards of their community.

CONTEST

THE "CONTEST" was well named; for she seemed in her early life to be racing a good part of the time, and met her end in an exciting but losing race with the Confederate cruiser "Alabama." Six months and fifteen days seems now a long time from New York to San Francisco and return, but at that time it was very fast going; one hundred days out, fifteen in port, and eighty home being the actual time consumed. One of her great joys was to outsail the "Trade Wind" of New York and the "Northern Light," of Boston. The Boston papers reported this close race, and the owners of the "Contest" stated that "If the owners of the 'Northern Light' feel inclined to bet on a race with the 'Contest', we will accommodate them."

In mentioning the time taken to get to California in clipper ship days, it is interesting to know that at the present time the trip from Boston to San Francisco is commonly made by the modern ships of the air in fourteen hours and fifteen minutes, elapsed time, i.e. including stops.

In 1863 took place an encounter between the "Contest" and the "Alabama." On a voyage from Yokohama bound for New York, the latter vessel appeared hoisting the American flag. A chase ensued and when the Southern vessel was within three miles she ran up the Confederate flag and sent a shot at the "Contest." From now on it was a test between steam and sail. The "Contest" continued to gain, but as the breeze died away the "Alabama" overhauled the Northern vessel. The Captain of the "Alabama" confessed that had the wind held strong the Northerner would have escaped. The victor captured all the provisions and everything of value and transferred all the crew to an English vessel from Liverpool which landed the men at Batavia, treating them with great kindness on the way. The insurance company was obliged to pay over $158,000 for the loss.

MERCHANTS' EXPRESS LINE
FOR
SAN FRANCISCO.

CURRENT RATES AND NO DECEPTION.

A 1 CLIPPER OF SATURDAY, DECEMBER 18.

Stowing and Handling with unusual care Shippers' Property

THE A 1 CLIPPER BARK

CONTEST

GEO. ALLEN, Master,

AT PIER 7, EAST RIVER.

This beautiful vessel has made the voyage to San Francisco, distancing the fleet sailing at the same time, and delivering her cargo without stain or damage to a single package. We feel confident that those who shipped before will give her the preference at this time. She will not be detained beyond Saturday, 18th inst. Early shipments will secure the most desirable places. Apply to

BABCOCK, COOLEY & CO.,
118 WATER ST., (Tontine Building.)

Messrs. DEWITT, KITTLE & CO., Agents in San Francisco.

NESBITT AND CO., PRINTERS.

Courtesy of Peabody Museum

CREMORNE

UNDOUBTEDLY pleasant memories led to giving this unusual name to an American clipper. Cremorne Gardens, a popular resort on the Thames, in Chelsea, a suburb of London, England, had probably been enjoyed by some one who had an opportunity to suggest a name for this speedy vessel which was built by Maxson, Fish & Co. at Mystic, Connecticut, in 1862. The namesake resort, formerly the estate of Viscount Cremorne, was sold and converted into a place of entertainment which attained its height of popularity between 1845 and 1877 and it was probably one of the places that seamen landing at London were likely to visit for relaxation after many weeks at sea.

According to "American Merchant Ships," that comprehensive book by Frederick C. Matthews, the "Magnificent Mystic Built Sharp Clipper Ship Cremorne," as she is described on the accompanying card advertising her sailing, had the rare distinction of being under the command of the same Captain — Charles H. Gates — during her whole sea life, which was unduly short. She completed six voyages from New York to San Francisco and on her seventh reached the latter port but on her return when bound for Liverpool, she disappeared and was never heard of thereafter, all 23 persons on board being lost. Captain Gates was a native of Mystic and one of four brothers, all deep-water shipmasters, and all of whom commanded Mystic-built ships during their careers. The son of Captain Charles Gates was mate with him on his last, ill-fated voyage.

The "Cremorne's" short life was marked by but one mishap of importance before her loss. She was partially dismasted off the River Plate while on her way to San Francisco in 1869 and had to finish the run under jury rig. The repairs made at San Francisco cost $5,000. Her first managing owners were Lawrence Giles & Co., and when that firm retired from business she came under the management of Pray & Dickens.

Courtesy of Peabody Museum

DERBY

THIS PICTURESQUE shipping card showing the famous horse race that is an annual event at Epsom Downs should have drawn the attention of would-be shippers. This announcement was indicative of the excellent passages made by the "Derby," which sailed almost every ocean race course known to the clippers of her day. She probably really was named for Elias Hasket Derby, but evidently the agents for the vessel believed they could attract more interest in this way. She was definitely a home vessel; for she was built by John Taylor at Chelsea for the well known shipping merchants Pickman, Silsbee et al. Her first voyage under Captain Samuel Hutchinson, Jr. took her to San Francisco, Hong Kong, Calcutta and then back to Boston, and through her life on the ocean she seems to have made use of San Francisco as a point of departure at least sixteen times. As Captain Hutchinson was her first commander, this advertised departure on Christmas day must have taken place early in her career.

The "Derby" was sold at San Francisco to George Howes & Co. in 1865, went under the German flag eleven years later and fourteen years afterwards became a Norwegian vessel. She is recorded as visiting this country as late as 1881.

This card recalls an unusual incident that happened at Epsom Downs on June 4th of the year 1913, the details of which have been sent us by the London office of the English-Speaking Union. During the suffragette movement Miss E. W. Davison, desirous of attracting attention to her cause, certainly carried out her intention. She deliberately ran onto the track during this Derby and threw herself against the King's entry "Anmer," putting him out of any possibility of winning. King George V and Queen Mary were present at the race, which was won by a horse called "Aboyeur." The suffragette who caused this commotion died in the Epsom Cottage Hospital a few days later.

DON QUIXOTE

THE OWNER of this interestingly named clipper, John Ellerton Lodge of Boston, great-grandfather of the present Senator Henry Cabot Lodge, like most people was familiar with this famous imaginary character when he chose to call this ship "Don Quixote," and when the Merchants Express Line advertised the sailing for San Francisco, the lion episode from Cervantes' popular work was chosen. This adventure, as one writer puts it, makes Don Quixote immortal when he declares: "Lion whelps to me! To me whelps of lions, and at such a time! Then, by God! those gentlemen who send them here shall see if I am a man to be frightened by lions." Don Diego tries to explain that these animals had not come to oppose him, but the knight-errant replies that he does not know whether the "gentlemen lions" had come to him or not, and demands that the keeper open the cage. Although frightened, the latter obeys. Again the translator marvels at the courage shown by Don Quixote and without motive. The latter springs from the saddle and to quote:

> Whilest the Keeper was opening the first Cage, Don Quixote began to consider, whether it were best to fight on foot, or on horsebacke: And at last he determined it should be on foot, fearing that Rozinante would bee afraid to looke upon the Lyons: and thereupon hee leap'd from his horse, cast by his Launce, buckled his Shield to him, and unsheathed his sword faire and softly; with a marvellous courage and valiant heart, he marched toward the Cart, recommending himselfe first to God, and then to his Lady Dulcinea. . . . The Keeper seeing Don Quixote in his posture, and that hee must needs let loose the Male Lyon, on paine of the bold Knight his indignation, he set the first Cage wide open, where the Lyon (as is saide) was, of an extraordinary bignesse, fearefull and ugly to see to. The first thing he did, was to tumble up and down the cage, stretch one pawe, and rowse himselfe, forthwith he yawned, and gently sneezed, then with his tongue some two handfuls long, he licked the dust out of his eyes, and washed his face; which done, he thrust his head out of the Cage, and looked round about him, with his eyes like fire coales: a sight and gesture able to make Temerity it selfe afraid. Onely Don Quixote beheld him earnestly, and wished he would leape out of the Cart, that they might grapple, for hee thought to slice him in pieces. Hitherto came the extreme

of his not-heard-of madnesse: but the generous Lyon, more courteous than arrogant, neglecting such childishnesse, and Bravados, after hee had looked round about him (as is said) turned his backe, and shewed his tayle to Don Quixote, and very quietly lay downe againe in the Cage.

The author figures that the lion was ashamed to injure the brave knight, whereupon the latter urged that the animal be provoked to come out, but the keeper convinced him not to do so. This odd scene ends with these words:

Well may Enchanters make mee unfortunate, but 'tis impossible they should bereave mee of my valour. . . . Well, if his Majesty chance to aske who it was that did it, tell him, The Knight of the Lyons: . . .

Cervantes' work contains over six hundred characters according to Carl T. Keller, and has been translated into more languages than any other book except the Bible, including odd tongues such as Esperanto, Hindu, Kashmiri, Turkish, Persian, Yiddish, Annamese, and Gujarati. He tells us that there are over 1300 editions, in 42 languages and dialects, of which he owned 730 copies now donated to Harvard.

This "World Renowned Out-and-Out Clipper Ship" came from the yard of Samuel Lapham in Medford, and her construction was supervised by Captain William Nott, who was her first captain and scheduled to command her on this advertised voyage to San Francisco. Nott spoke of her "as being as good as she was beautiful." Other commanders were Elwell, Hall, Ellery and Johnson. On two occasions she took on board Chinese passengers from two wrecked vessels. She was a quite frequent visitor to Boston.

In 1864 the "Don Quixote" was sold to a firm in Havre and ten years later she came into possession of other owners at that same port. Her record was an unusual one and even after traveling over the globe for more than twenty years, Lloyd's still classed her as "A1."

Don Quixote's traveling companion, Esquire Sancho Panza, also had a ship named for him, described later in this brochure.

Courtesy of H. W. Peabody & Co., Boston, Mass.

EAGLE WING

CAPTAIN EBEN H. LINNELL had charge of this beautiful extreme clipper on most of her voyages from the time of launching at the Curtis yard at Medford, until 1864 when a heavy squall suddenly parted the boom tackle, causing the spanker boom to sweep across the deck, throwing Linnell so heavily against the wheel that he died shortly after. On the run from Foo Chow to London the log contains some curious spelling, for whoever was delegated by Captain Linnell to keep the records had a curious method of making his entries. He wrote of the "heaviest of wather . . . sea hove up in grate confushion" . . . and, when passing the Straits of Sunday, the diary reads, "Strates." Evidently the keeper of the log on the day before Christmas of 1853 was more familiar with spelling. He records this dangerous situation: "Hove ship to under close reefed main topsail and spencer, ship lying with lee rail under water, nearly on beam ends . . . it blowing a perfect hurricane . . . in 31 years at sea have never seen a typhoon or hurricane so severe. Had two men washed overboard, saved one; . . ."

On a voyage from Boston to Bombay in 1865 she disappeared and was never heard from. Chase & Tappan of Boston were her owners.

James O. Curtis, who built this clipper, commenced shipbuilding in 1839 at the yard off Swan Street, Medford, Mass., eventually launching a total of 78 vessels, including the "Ocean Express" and the "Bunker Hill" also mentioned in this brochure.

THE BEST SHIP LOADING!
Coleman's California Line for San Francisco.

THE A 1 EXTREME CLIPPER SHIP

EMERALD ISLE

CORNISH, Commander,
Is now rapidly loading at Pier 15 E. R., foot of Wall St.

This magnificent Clipper Ship is one of the fastest sailers afloat. Has made the passage to Liverpool in same time as Steamer "America," she has three decks, superior ventilation, and is in every way a first-class ship. We invite shippers to inspect this vessel, and send their goods alongside immediately. We expect this ship will beat the fleet now loading. For balance of Freight, apply to

WM. T. COLEMAN & CO., 161 Pearl St., near Wall.

Agents in San Francisco, Messrs. WM. T. COLEMAN & CO.

NESBITT & CO., PRINTERS.

Courtesy of Peabody Museum

EMERALD ISLE

THIS EXTREME CLIPPER was built by Trufant, Drummond & Co. in their yard at the north end of the City of Bath, Maine, near the foot of Trufant Street, which was named for the senior partner of this enterprising firm, Gilbert C. Trufant. The original owners of this, the largest ship built at Bath up to that time, were W. & J. Tapscott of New York and on her maiden voyage she was under command of Captain Cornish.

Trufant, Drummond & Co. turned out a total of 27 vessels, including the "Monsoon," "Viking," "Windward" and "Mary Robinson." The "Emerald Isle" was the fourteenth ship built by them.

Not much information seems to be available about this clipper in addition to the above, except that in 1885 she was listed under Dutch ownership, having been renamed the "Barendina Oriria," hailing from Batavia.

"How do you know she's a Yankee clipper;
    Blow, boys, blow!
Because her masts and yards shine like silver,
    Blow, my bully boys, blow!"

"From AMERICAN SEA SONGS & CHANTEYS
From the Days of Iron Men and Wooden Ships,"
Edited by Frank Shay, Illustrated by Edward A. Wilson, W. W. Norton & Co. Inc., 1948.

EMPRESS OF THE SEAS

WHILE THE CARD which accompanies this story has the name "Empress of the Sea," her real name was as given in the heading. Apparently the printer misjudged the space when making up the card and did not have room for the final "s." This clipper, which Carl Cutler has referred to as "one of the beautiful creatures" and a "famous princess of the blood," was built at East Boston in 1853 by Donald McKay. Her bow was ornamented with a full length female figure in white garments, the left hand extended holding a globe, while the right hand, reposing by her side, held the sceptre of the seas. Bought when about half completed by William Wilson & Son of Baltimore for $125,000, at various times she was commanded by Captains Putnam, Oakford, Halcy, Francis W. Wilson (at one time her first mate), and William B. Cobb of Brewster, Mass. First used in the California trade, she was later operated between England and Australia in the White Star Line. On December 19th, 1861, she was burned at Queenscliff Bight, Port Phillip, Australia, becoming a total loss.

The "Empress of the Seas" was apparently the type of clipper which one newspaper described as "just the kind of vehicle, or whatever else it may be called, that a sensible man would choose for a ninety-day voyage."

Courtesy of American Antiquarian Society

FRANKLIN

THE SAILING ANNOUNCEMENT of the superior clipper "Franklin" is an interesting one, for in addition to showing Benjamin Franklin conducting his kite experiment, the owners of the vessel believed the mode of conveyance of that day so assured that they dared picture a train and engine on the same card.

Roger Amory some years ago assumed the investment business of the old shipping firm of Wm. F. Weld & Co., and among his papers is the original log of this ship from which he has been good enough to make a number of notations. She was built in 1859 by Paul Curtis in East Boston, and sold thirteen years later to W. H. Kinsman, whose place of business was at 3 India Street, Boston. Her log shows no particularly interesting entries until the year 1870, when the "Franklin" sailed into Boston Harbor and was towed to Tudor's Ice Wharf in Charlestown to take on ice for shipment to Batavia. It will be remembered that Frederic Tudor was a pioneer in sending this commodity to the West Indies, East Indies, and even Calcutta, India. On this occasion 1212 tons were taken on board. A further entry speaks of arriving four months later at Batavia where 800 tons were "turned out." Whether the remainder was deposited at other ports or whether it had melted is not mentioned. In addition she carried oil and rosin on this voyage, her other cargoes at times being rice and sugar.

Paul Curtis established himself in 1839 at the yard on South Street, Medford, Mass., at the end of Curtis Street. In 1852 he transferred his operations to a yard on Porter Street, East Boston. At one time he also used the shipyard on Riverside Avenue, Medford, Mass., opposite the end of Park Street, which was established in 1803 by Thatcher Magoun. One hundred ninety-three vessels in all were built at this yard.

The "Bostonian," mentioned earlier, had a full-length figurehead of Benjamin Franklin, showing that eminent patriot with a continental hat under his left arm and a manuscript in his right hand. This figurehead would have been more appropriate for the "Franklin" but was probably selected for the "Bostonian" because Franklin was one of Boston's most celebrated natives.

While writing of figureheads, it might be interesting to mention that it is said that the American ship "Commodore T. H. Allen" was the only vessel to have a figurehead of a man smoking a cigar!

The illustrious person for whom the "Franklin" was named descended from the Folgers of Nantucket, as is well known, and Samuel E. Morison with his usual cleverness wrote that "Ben's keel was laid in Nantucket, but the old lady went to Boston to launch him."

★　　★　　★

GAMECOCK

IT IS quite appropriate that Samuel Hall of East Boston, the builder of this vessel and Samuel H. Pook, her designer, should choose for the figurehead a fighting cock with outstretched neck and head looking as if he were eager for a fight and anxious to poke his guiding countenance into almost every important port in the world. It was also equally appropriate that James Smith & Son, Agents, should use a similar figure on this rare announcement of her sailing for San Francisco.

Although not one of the fastest of clippers, the "Gamecock" made a wonderful showing when going to windward and in spite of suffering the loss of sails and topsails, during her long career of thirty years, she made many speedy voyages to distant places, including Colombo, San Francisco, Honolulu, Hong Kong, Shanghai, Bombay, Callao, Bangkok, Singapore, Melbourne and Manila. She was one of the clippers upon which many wagers were made at the Astor House in New York or at

FOR

SAN FRANCISCO,

DIRECT.

Empire Line---With Quick Dispatch.

NEW CLIPPER SHIP

GAME COCK,

Loading at Pier 9, East River.

It is believed this elegant Ship will accomplish the voyage in less time than it has ever yet been made.

Shippers are desired to examine her before engaging elsewhere.

For Freight, apply to

JAMES SMITH & SON.

Courtesy of Clark Collection, Francis Russell Hart Nautical Museum, Massachusetts Institute of Technology

the Merchants Exchange in Boston, and on one occasion was one of three clippers to arrive at San Francisco within one day of each other. Her captains were Clement, Jayne, Hollis, Sherburn, Osgood, Williams, and Stoddard. She left Boston on her first voyage in 1851 and was finally condemned at the Cape of Good Hope.

The "Gamecock" was built for Captain Daniel C. Bacon of Barnstable, later one of Boston's leading sea captains and a most successful merchant. At a very early age, he set out for Boston on an old white horse to seek a position on some vessel. As he was proceeding through the outskirts of the city, some boys yelled at him "bushwhacker." Young Bacon dismounted, handed them something in return and then continued on his way. After a life on the ocean he became interested in building and owning a number of vessels for himself, or for himself and his son, W. B. Bacon. He superintended their construction and the writer of his private biography, Julia Bacon, his granddaughter, remembers being told that his son used to drive with him to Medford or East Boston to follow the work, inspecting every detail. Doubtless he often journeyed to Hall's shipyard in the latter place to view the progress of the "Gamecock." This same biographer was told her grandfather often visited a friend in the suburbs of Boston who always kept in his room a coffin in which he desired to be buried, leaving orders that when his funeral took place he should be carried out by the back door. Julia Bacon also recalls that a model of the beautiful clipper was among the objects of interest at the first anniversary of the Cape Cod Associates.

Captain Bacon was President of the American Navigation Club and when in 1852 he sent a challenge to the ship builders of Great Britain, it was supposed that the "Gamecock" inspired the challenge and would probably have been the ship selected for the contest. Baring Bros. of London were the agents in these negotiations which came to naught.

No story of the "Gamecock" would be complete without a short account of her owner and his residences. The old Bacon homestead was situated in Barnstable and was built in 1642 by Nathaniel Bacon, the earliest ancestor in this country of Captain Daniel C. Bacon. Another Bacon house, built in 1832 by Captain Bacon to replace the earlier one, was occupied by the family until recent years when it was sold to Messrs. Allan P. Chase and Francis F. Chase, of Chase, Parker & Co. Inc., Boston, and is now used as an Inn. Francis Chase has a pleasure yacht — a reconditioned navy crash boat — which he named "Game-cock" after the original Bacon clipper. Another interesting item concerning the old Bacon farm is that there is a marker on the property indicating the site of the blockhouse which was used by the original settlers to withstand attacks by hostile Indians. Behind the house in Temple Place, Boston, occupied by Daniel C. Bacon, was a garden running down to the alley-way leading from Temple Place to West Street.

Captain Bacon, and later his son Francis, owned Clyde Park, Brookline, now the property of The Country Club. It was disposed of by Francis Bacon as being too far from Boston. "Toadside" and "Frogmore" were two curiously named family residences in Jamaica Plain near Jamaica Pond.

A number of stories about Captain Bacon were narrated in the Trust Company's pamphlet "Some Merchants and Sea Captains of Old Boston," now out of print. In the Captain's diary appeared an amusing record not previously mentioned: "March 12, 1811, Saw a land bird which I think must be out of his reckoning, or I must, but I think I shall find mine more correct."

★　　★　　★

GARIBALDI

It was quite fitting that the name of that famous Italian patriot, Giuseppe Garibaldi, should be given to an American clipper ship, as heroes of fights for independence have always been admired in this country. Garibaldi also had a close connection with the sea, as he had once served in the Sardinian navy. He plotted, with a number of companions, to seize the frigate on which they were serving and then to occupy the arsenal of

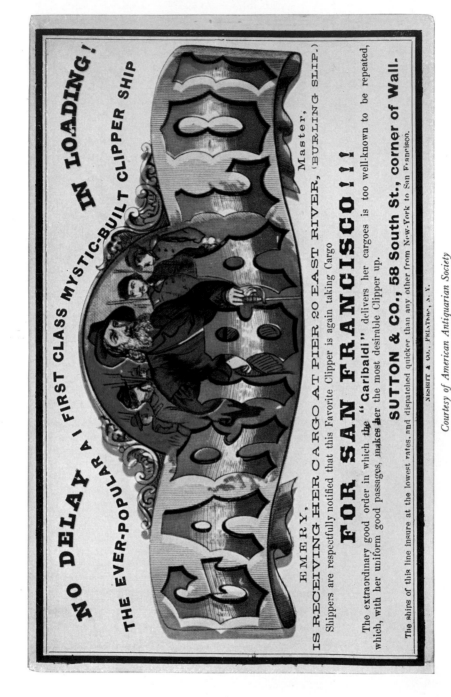

Courtesy of American Antiquarian Society

Genoa. The plot was discovered and Garibaldi, who fortunately evaded capture, was condemned to death by default. He later escaped to South America and was given letters-of-marque by the State of Rio Grande do Sul which had revolted against Brazil.

While we could not find any information about the Captain Emery mentioned on the accompanying card, it is interesting to know that in her later years of service the "Garibaldi" was commanded by Captain Samuel H. Thacher of Yarmouth, Cape Cod, Massachusetts, where he died in 1901. Thacher is one of the best known names in that town. Judging by letters he wrote to the owners while he was in command, by that time the "Garibaldi" was in very poor condition, leaking almost continuously and with masts in such bad shape that there was constant fear that they would not last through a voyage. The "Garibaldi" at that time was under the ownership of Howes & Crowell of Boston. Thacher also commanded two other ships under the same ownership — the "Valley Forge" and the "Carrolton." He later engaged in the coastwise trade as captain of the "Albert Schultz," "Puritan," "R. S. Spofford," and the "John Twohy." The last named ship was built for him and he remained in command up to the time when his failing health led to his retirement, thus ending a maritime career which he began at the age of 14.

Mention of Cape Cod skippers, brings to mind this verse, with which they were all probably familiar, from "American Sea Songs and Chanteys, From the Days of Iron Men and Wooden Ships," Edited by Frank Shay, Illustrated by Edward A. Wilson, W. W. Norton & Co. Inc., 1948.

> "Cape Cod cats they have no tails,
> Heave away!   Heave away!
> They lost them all in sou'east gales,
> We're bound for Californiay!"

GEORGE PEABODY

THIS VESSEL was named for George Peabody, long a resident of London, and not for the merchant of the same name, son of Joseph Peabody of Salem, according to L. W. Jenkins of the Peabody Museum of Salem. The former Peabody was an international banker and philanthropist and it was only quite natural that William F. Weld, whose reputation as a ship merchant was equally well known in most of the important ports of the world, should have named one of his many ships for the better known of the two men. The details of this vessel's career are recorded in the log in the office of Roger Amory. She was built in 1854 by J. O. Curtis of Medford and sold nineteen years later for $45,000. She is advertised as having three decks.

George Peabody's career could be reviewed many times, as it was such an unusual one. Even to enumerate his thoughtful and generous deeds would take a larger pamphlet than William Dismore Chapple required when he wrote the life of this benefactor for the Peabody Museum of Salem. It would seem only natural to name a clipper for a man who gave a library to Danvers; who gave to Baltimore (where he had lived for twenty years of his early business life) funds for the erection of the Peabody Institute; who gave many houses in London to help thousands of the poor of that city, still known as the Peabody Buildings; for one who was offered a decoration by Queen Victoria, but declined it; who established an Education Fund for our Southern and Southwestern States; who gave Georgetown (Massachusetts) a Memorial Church and a library; who donated the Peabody Museum of Salem, a library at Thetford, Vermont (where he lived for a year), and also one at Newburyport; who gave funds for a museum of natural history at Yale and also funds for a museum of archaeology and anthropology at Harvard.

This American lived and transacted business in London, and when he died the Londoners desired that he be buried in West-

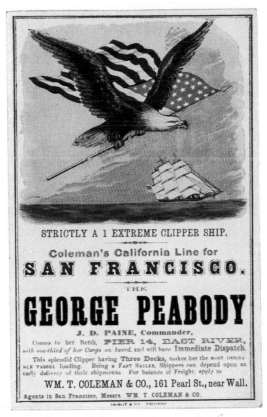

Courtesy of American Antiquarian Society

minster Abbey. Although not buried there, funeral services were held for him and were attended by Royalty, the Lord Mayor of London and many distinguished personages. We understand that the burial place prepared for him is still to be seen there near the grave of the Unknown Soldier.

George Peabody's gifts were unusual and so was his life and his business career. He was born in 1795 in the South Parish of Danvers, later named Peabody for its distinguished citizen; not particularly well educated; an apprentice in the grocery business, then in the draper business in Newburyport with his older brother David; driven out by the Newburyport fire, whereupon he and his Uncle John set up a dry goods store in Georgetown, near Washington, in 1812. He enlisted in the defense of Washington, formed the firm of Riggs & Peabody, and although he put in only $1,650.40 of capital he built up the merchandise business, removed to Baltimore in 1822 and started branches in Philadelphia and New York, and went to England to sell cotton when thirty-two years of age. While in London he became one of the leading bankers, negotiated a loan to the State of Maryland, returning a commission of $60,000. For thirty-three years he resided in London, conducting international banking, and becoming one of the foremost if not the foremost American then in Europe. Riggs & Peabody suffered reverses, and in 1843 the firm was styled George Peabody & Company, merchants and bankers, lending large sums of money on easy terms.

His Fourth of July banquets in London were famous, the first one being attended by the Duke of Wellington, then eighty-four years of age. At the time of the First International Exposition in London he paid the expenses which the United States refused to pay, but later this sum was refunded. At a great dinner at the London Coffee House, frequented by Benjamin Franklin, Queen Victoria loaned her portrait, which was placed next to Stuart's painting of Washington. A loving cup from America, inscribed "Francis Peabody of Salem to George Peabody of London, 1851," was passed around. He was given the freedom of the city and there is a statue of him near the Royal Exchange, a replica of which is in Baltimore. He was also awarded a Gold Medal by our Congress.

At the 100th Anniversary of the separation of Danvers from Salem he presented another Peabody Institute to that part of Danvers now called Peabody.

In 1854 he took into partnership Junius S. Morgan and two years later his son, J. Pierpont Morgan, aged nineteen, asked for a job and was accepted. Later on the latter formed his own firm.

When Peabody revisited his native town in 1856 he had already become the chief financial representative of America in London. Edward Everett at that time declared that he "turned paper into gold," but he was not satisfied until he had donated most of his possessions to charity and worthy causes. He was of course received at Danvers with a grand reception.

One year later took place the fearful panic when many firms failed, but by borrowing four million dollars his firm came through the crisis.

He never married, but the name of George Peabody will live forever on both sides of the Atlantic. His death took place in London in 1869 and by his will he wished to be buried in Harmony Grove Cemetery in Salem. England sent him home in her newest warship, the "Monarch," convoyed by the American man-of-war "Plymouth." They arrived at Portland, Maine, and then a locomotive, renamed temporarily "George Peabody," drew the remains to the town of Peabody. Many dignitaries were present at this service, including Queen Victoria's representative Prince Arthur, later the Duke of Connaught. George Peabody made the remark during the last part of his life that he had not sought to relieve pauperism but to prevent it. Gladstone said that he "taught men how to use money and how not to be its slave." A railroad station agent referred to him in these odd words: "He was a comfortable man to have around and would have been popular if he had not been worth a dollar."

A fitting end to this chapter would be the two verses dedicated to him a few years before his death, written by Oliver Wendell Holmes:

Bankrupt! our pockets inside out!
    Empty of words to speak his praises!
Worcester and Webster up the spout!
    Dead broke of laudatory phrases!
Yet why with flowery speeches tease,
    With vain superlatives distress him?
Has language better words than these?
    The Friend Of All His Race, God Bless Him!

A simple prayer — but words more sweet
    By human lips were never uttered,
Since Adam left the country seat
    Where angel wings around him fluttered.
The old look on with tear-dimmed eyes,
    The children cluster to caress him,
And every voice unbidden cries
    The Friend Of All His Race, God Bless Him!

GRACE DARLING

APPARENTLY the fame of this English heroine of 1838 persisted until 1854 with enough popular interest to lead to the naming of one of the last of the extreme clipper ships for her. As her exploit had to do with the saving of lives at sea, it was quite fitting that she should be further recognized in this way.

It was in September of 1838 that the "Forfarshire" with 63 persons aboard struck on the Farne Islands, off the coast of England, 43 being drowned. William Darling, father of Grace, was then the keeper of the Longstone lighthouse on the islet of that name, one of the group of Farne Islands. By a rare demonstration of courage, strength and skill, the father and daughter reached the wreck and brought four men and a woman to the lighthouse. Grace and her father received the gold medal of the Humane Society, and other honors, for their bravery in this daring rescue.

The "Grace Darling" was another of the clippers built by E. and H. O. Briggs of Boston. She was said to be a favorite with shippers and was singularly free from the accidents so common with clipper ships of her day. Her figurehead quite appropriately was a female attired in white garments. Her commander on her initial voyage was Captain S. H. Doane and her first owner was C. B. Fessenden, commission merchant, located at 134 State Street, Boston. Fessenden sold her to Baker & Morrill, also of Boston, in 1858. The partners in this firm were Ezra H. Baker and C. J. Morrill, with offices at 31 Commercial Street. Among her other commanders were Captain Allen H. Bearse, Baxter, and Gibbs. In 1868 she was sold to Adams, Blinn & Co. and was used in the lumber trade in the Pacific.

TO SAIL ON OR BEFORE THURSDAY, MAY 19, 1864.

Glidden & Williams' Line

FOR SAN FRANCISCO.

K.ILMAN & MALLORY SC.

THE BEAUTIFUL EXTREME CLIPPER SHIP

Grace Darling,

CAPT. ALLEN H. BEARSE.

This ship is well known to the trade as one of the fastest of the clipper fleet,
always delivering her Cargoes in fine order.
Shippers will please send forward their goods promptly.

☞ *For Freight, apply at the California Packet Office,*
No. 114 STATE STREET....BOSTON.

Woman's Press.

Courtesy of Herbert G. Porter

GREAT REPUBLIC

THERE WAS great excitement at Donald McKay's yard in East Boston on the day, October 4, 1853, when this builder's masterpiece was launched. Special trains conveyed spectators from all parts of Massachusetts and elsewhere to witness this event. It has been estimated that at least 30,000 people crossed the harbor by the East Boston ferry, and every point of vantage was crowded with interested persons. Those who were superstitious would doubtless believe that the use of Cochituate water to christen her, in lieu of something stronger, brought on her the ill luck that overtook her in New York a short time afterwards, the day after Christmas, only a few days before she was scheduled to set out for Liverpool. A fire broke out on Front Street and the blazing cinders spread to this grand vessel. Having four decks it proved impossible to scuttle her completely, as the water was too shallow to cover the upper deck. McKay, heavy of heart, decided to hand her over to the underwriters, who settled the claim for $180,000. for the vessel itself and $275,000. for the cargo. This largest merchant sailing vessel, built by this great builder, never had an opportunity really to show her speed under the large sail plan carried on the four masts. Her cabin and staterooms were the most luxurious up to that time.

A. A. Low & Brother bought the damaged hull and engaged that noted captain, N. B. Palmer of Stonington, to refit her under a smaller rig. The upper deck was never replaced, and she sailed for Liverpool in February, 1855. Captain Limeburner, whose name appears on this very simple, but very rare sailing card, commanded her on this run and stated that she behaved nobly. This card is reproduced from a picture in Richard C. McKay's book "Some Famous Sailing Ships and Their Builder Donald McKay," which was taken from the original owned by Miss M. Limeburner, granddaughter of Captain Limeburner.

FOR

SAN FRANCISCO

***

THE CELEBRATED CLIPPER SHIP

GREAT REPUBLIC

LIMEBURNER, Commander,

AT PIER 36 EAST RIVER,

Will have immediate dispatch.

This ship has been newly coppered, and put in complete order. Her short passages, and the perfect delivery of cargoes, entitle her to a preference with shippers. Having large hatches, she can take bulky freight under deck. Two-thirds of her capacity is already engaged.

For balance of Freight, apply to

A. A. Low & Brothers,

31 Burling Slip.

From "Some Famous Sailing Ships and Their Builder, Donald McKay"
by Richard C. McKay

The French Government chartered her for use in the Mediterranean at Marseilles, and she then returned to our merchant service, making some excellent runs in spite of her reduced rig. Off the Falkland Islands a huge sea caved in some deck beams, causing the provisions to be ruined. With famine threatening, she put in at Falkland Islands, later continuing her voyage to London. She was held by New York authorities in 1861, as many of the shares were owned by Southerners whose interests were soon purchased by the Low firm. In 1866 she was bought by residents of Yarmouth, Nova Scotia — Liverpool later became her home port. On a voyage from Rio to St. John, New Brunswick, she sprung a bad leak and had to be abandoned, the crew reaching Bermuda safely.

A. A. Low, the great New York merchant, was the son of Seth Low of Gloucester, Mass. He started out as a clerk for a Salem merchant, then went to Canton as clerk for Russell & Co., the largest American firm in China. In four years he was admitted to partnership and remained with them for three more years. He then returned to New York and founded his own business, which became the great house of A. A. Low & Brother. His firm was one of the first to do business with Japan when that country was opened for trade in 1860. Thus the enterprise of another New Englander made itself felt in important national and international affairs!

remarkable man; otherwise there would have been no survivors. He was a New-Englander of the best sea-going stock of the old capable times . . . With ten days' provisions Captain Josiah Mitchell performed this memorable voyage of forty-three days and eight hours in an open boat, sailing four thousand miles in reality and thirty-three hundred and sixty by direct courses, and brought every man safe to land. A bright, simple-hearted, un-assuming, plucky, and most companionable man. I walked the deck with him twenty-eight (twenty-five) days — when I was not copying diaries — and I remember him with reverent honor." The narrator also wrote: "It is an amazing adventure. There is nothing of its sort in history that surpasses it in im-possibilities made possible . . . The interest of this story is un-quenchable, it is of the sort that time cannot decay." The Captain's physician on the voyage home said of Mitchell, "Again had this intrepid captain, by sheer force of will and indomitable courage, stood Death off until his object had been accomplished."

The disaster, which occurred just after rounding Cape Horn, was caused by the mate who, contrary to orders, went below deck with a lantern to draw some varnish. He also neglected after the explosion to close the bung of the cask. In a few minutes fire had spread so rapidly that the men had to take to the three boats, saving only a small quantity of provisions and water. The Captain, who had with him fifteen men, reached Hawaii, but no trace was found of the other two boats. Copies of the graphic diaries of Captain Mitchell and the two Ferguson brothers (combined in one story) were loaned to us by Lawrence W. Jenkins of the Peabody Museum of Salem. They are exceed-ingly rare and particularly interesting from the fact that they were presented by Mrs. E. S. Ferguson. The food of the unfor-tunate sixteen at the start consisted of two crackers and a pint of water and their sufferings were intense, but they did not have to resort to killing one of their number, "*Le dernier ressort*," as happened after the loss of the whaler "Essex," which was sunk by a whale. Henry Ferguson described their discomforts in their cramped quarters and the trying weather conditions, which he referred to as follows: "Never saw, never felt, never heard, never experienced such heat, such darkness, such lightning and thunder and wind and rain, in my life before." Upon arrival the Captain noted, "a famished starved set of men . . . Not a man could walk." Curiously enough no one died. As for the rations, wrote Henry Ferguson, "The ham-rags are not gone yet, and the boot-legs, we find, are very palatable after we get the salt out of them." One of their last meals consisted of a canvas cover to the ham bone, which was divided into fifteen portions, and the staves from an oaken butter tub. The diary then goes on to explain that "we ate nothing except the soft straps of two pairs of boots, three on the 39th day and saved one for the 40th, (their last meal). After arrival the Captain tried to eat some clam broth. When it did not agree with him, he said, "Strange I can't keep that nice broth down, after eating my boot tops and digesting them! However, conditions were somewhat different then." When it seemed as if he could not last through the voyage, he said, "Don't worry doctor; I'll make it, I'll live till I see my Susie." (Should be "Katie"; "Susie" was his first wife.) Their sense of humor stayed with them, however; for speaking of this leather diet, Ferguson said that "one of the men told me he was obliged to eat a pair of boots which were so old and rotten that they were full of holes; and then he smiled gently and said he didn't know, though, but what the holes tasted about as good as the balance of the boot." As another example of their pluck Ferguson wrote that "they used to spend hours together describing delicious dinners they had eaten at home, and earnestly planning interminable and preposterous bills of fare for dinners they were going to eat on shore, if they ever lived through their troubles to do it, poor fellows. The Captain said plain bread and butter would be good enough for him all the days of his life, if he could only get it." And again he recalled that "Images of food and niceties are ever recurring to our minds and we think with remorse of how much we have wasted when we had plenty." Often he said, we "dreamed — and always of such feasts! bread, and fowls, and meat—everything a man could think of, piled upon long tables, and smoking hot! And we sat down and seized upon the first dish in our reach like ravenous wolves, and carried it to our lips and — then we woke up and found the same starving comrades about us, and the vacant sky and the desolate sea!"

The third day before the last on the water was the Captain's birthday and Henry made this entry: "Toward evening saw a magnificent rainbow — the first we had seen. Captain said, 'Cheer up, boys; it's a prophecy — it's the bow of promise'." On the following morning, June 15, land was sighted. They made a landing in the only possible place and were carried ashore by the Kanaka men and women, who almost killed them with kindness. Purses of gold were also raised, causing the Captain to remark that he felt like a criminal upon receiving it. "There is some true charity in the world yet," he declared. They convalesced at beautiful Hilo. They fell in with the Governess of Hawaii and suite, described by Henry as "mighty ugly, fat and about 300 lbs. tonnage."

The ill-fated "Hornet," as well as its captain, hailed from Freeport, Maine, which is noted for its unique "Desert of Maine" composed of many acres of beautiful sand, visited by thousands of vacationists. This vessel has been described as a hold-over clipper of the extreme type, and finely constructed. Two years after launching, she raced the record-making "Flying Cloud" to San Francisco, being beaten only by one hour. As the name of Mitchell appears on this shipping announcement and as two other voyages to San Francisco are mentioned, it is probable that this card advertised the actual ill-fated and last voyage of this clipper.

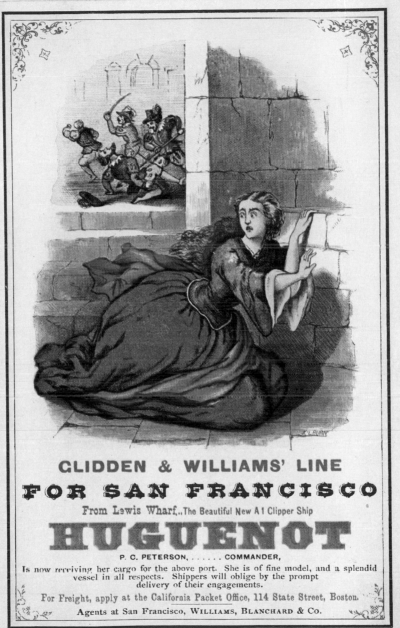

Courtesy of American Antiquarian Society

HUGUENOT

PRESUMABLY a friend of one of the owners of Glidden & Williams, Inc. was a descendant of a French Huguenot who may have escaped from the persecutions at La Rochelle, the Island of Ré and elsewhere in France and for this reason this name was chosen for the new clipper about to sail for California. This card shows a woman who has escaped from the massacre that took place after the revocation of the Edict of Nantes in 1685. The result was a benefit to New England; for prior to 1716 over four thousand *émigrés* came to this part of the country and to a great extent to the eastern part of Massachusetts. Perhaps, even, the namer of this vessel may have been a relative or had in mind a member of the Revere, Faneuil, Bowdoin, Marquand, Sigourney, Bernon, Mercier, Allaire, Beauchamp, Chardon, Dupee, Dumaresq, Mascarene, Olivier, Rawlins, or other families. The Huguenot influence on New England life is too well known to need repetition. Cotton Mather said of them: "They challenge a room in our best affections. The little company of Huguenots that settled in Boston brought with them qualities that were needed at that day. They brought a buoyancy and a cheerfulness that must have been contagious. And the mispronounced names from beyond the seas that stand out so boldly on the pages of its history — names such as Bowdoin and Faneuil and Revere — recall in the flight of the Huguenot to these shores an episode not only pathetic but important also for its bearing upon social and public life and typical character in New England."

Under Captain Sylvanus Nickerson the "Huguenot" foundered in the Indian Ocean on her voyage from Hilo to Boston laden with sugar, sinking in three hours. Her captain and crew succeeded in reaching shore on an island in the Ormbay Straits, where they were made prisoners by the Malays, who released them. They then made their way to another island, being finally rescued by a Dutch man-of-war.

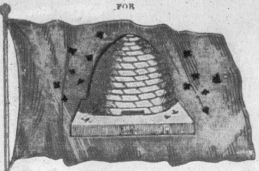

From the collection of the State Street Trust Company

JOHN GILPIN

JOHN GILPIN is synonymous with speed, but the vessel of this name did not travel a bit faster than the subject of Cowper's well known and amusing poem entitled "The Diverting History of John Gilpin, Showing How He Went Farther Than He Intended, And Came Safe Home Again." This poetry was sung by most of the children of an earlier generation, the first stanza of which was:

> John Gilpin was a citizen
> Of credit and renown,
> A train-band captain eke was he
> Of famous London town.

There not being room enough in the chaise for the whole family on the wedding anniversary of himself and his wife, the husband was urged to ride to town on a steed. That he was not a horseman will be seen:—

> So stooping down, as needs he must
> Who cannot sit upright,
> He grasp'd the mane with both his hands,
> And eke with all his might.

> His horse, who never in that sort
> Had handled been before,
> What thing upon his back had got
> Did wonder more and more.

As he galloped along he said to himself:—

> . . — It is my wedding-day,
> And all the world would stare,
> If wife should dine at Edmonton
> And I should dine at Ware!

A braying ass "did sing most loud and clear"—

> Whereat his horse did snort, as he
> Had heard a lion roar,
> And gallop'd off with all his might,
> As he had done before.

Those he met yelled at the rider—

> Stop thief! — a highwayman!
> Not one of them was mute;
> And all and each that pass'd that way
> Did join in the pursuit.

Believing Gilpin was riding a race the turnpike gates were flung open and the poetry continued—

> And so he did — and won it too! —
>   For he got first to town;
> Nor stopp'd till where he had got up
>   He did again get down.

The poetry finishes with—

> Now let us sing — Long live the king,
>   And Gilpin long live he;
> And, when he next doth ride abroad,
>   May I be there to see!

The "John Gilpin" had a number of races around the Horn, particularly a world-famous sweepstakes with four entries. Richard C. McKay well describes this noted event—

> Like steeds that know their riders, they were handled with the most exquisite skill and judgment, and in such hands they bounded out upon the "glad waters" most gracefully. Each, being put upon her mettle from the start, was driven, under the seaman's whip and spur, at full speed over a course that it would take them three long months to run.

The "John Gilpin" finished second. Four hundred seamen participated.

This sailing card is probably copied from the stern piece of this clipper which represented John Gilpin in the same uncomfortable attitude shown here. She was a Boston product, designed and constructed by Samuel Hall for the well known merchants Pierce & Hunnewell, and often returned to her home port. She met her end in 1857 or 1858 in an unusual manner; for under Captain John F. Ropes, on her way to New Bedford with whale oil, she ran into a submerged iceberg and had to be abandoned. As those aboard went over the side, fire broke out, completing her unfortunate finish. Several years later a vessel from New Bedford picked up a cask of oil from this wrecked vessel 2780 miles from where she sank.

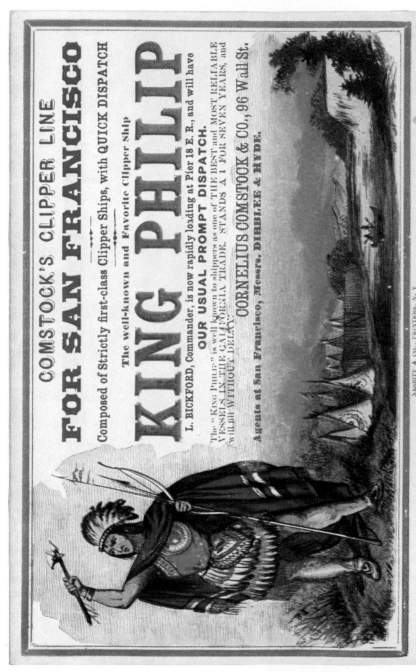

COMSTOCK'S CLIPPER LINE

FOR SAN FRANCISCO

Composed of Strictly first-class Clipper Ships, with QUICK DISPATCH

The well-known and Favorite Clipper Ship

KING PHILIP

L. BICKFORD, Commander, is now rapidly loading at Pier 18 E. R., and will have

OUR USUAL PROMPT DISPATCH.

The "King Philip" is well known to shippers as one of THE BEST and MOST RELIABLE VESSELS IN THE CALIFORNIA TRADE. STANDS A 1 FOR SEVEN YEARS, and will be WITHOUT DELAY.

CORNELIUS COMSTOCK & CO., 96 Wall St.

Agents at San Francisco, Messrs. DIBBLEE & HYDE.

NESBITT & CO., PRINTERS, N. Y.

Courtesy of Bostonian Society

KING PHILIP

PATRICK GRANT and Wm. B. Reynolds, the owners of this clipper, instead of choosing one of the friendly Indians such as Samoset, Massasoit, Squanto, Hobomok, or others, to carry their name, selected King Philip, the most warlike of the tribe and one of the last chieftains to succumb to the new arrivals here. Doubtless they came at this decision for the reason that the vessel of this name would be battling the elements on the ocean as this Indian had battled the whites for many years on land.

The first voyage of this clipper, whose figurehead we have used on the cover of this brochure, seems to have been in 1854 soon after having been turned out from the less known yard of George Thomas of Quincy at Quincy Point on the site now occupied by the modern plant of the Procter & Gamble Manufacturing Company. Asa Eldridge was in command. There seems to have been another ship of this name but spelled with two "l's," for which Glidden & Williams were agents. This card evidently announced the first named clipper seven years after construction.

A brief outline of this namesake Chieftain's career might fit in well with this chapter. It is almost certain that in 1665 King Philip found his way to Nantucket in an unsuccessful attempt to slay one of his tribe who he claimed had profaned the name of one of his relatives. His first experience with the Pilgrims was in 1671 when the Commissioners met him and his councillors at Taunton, an occasion described as "unrivalled in picturesqueness," and again an historian wrote that "Never before or since did the plain roof of a New England Meeting House cover a contrast so highly colored in costume and idea." An agreement, not fulfilled, was made to deliver the arms of the tribe to the English. He later journeyed to Plymouth and also to Boston to try to explain why more weapons had not been delivered. He then insisted that he was a subject of the King of England and not of the Colonies, declaring "When he comes I am ready." Three years later, in 1675, war broke out and villages were pillaged and the colonists under Benjamin Church chased the enemy into the Narragansett country. Philip and three thousand brave warriors fortified an island in a large swamp at Kingston, Rhode Island, and provisioned themselves for the winter. Here, on the 19th of December, 1675, took place one of the most decisive battles ever fought for possession of these lands. A friendly Indian gave away the location, a bloody battle took place and the Indians were driven out and their wigwams destroyed. Our troops suffered terribly and were obliged to march eighteen miles on a severe night. Many of their men were badly wounded. Philip and some of his warriors, however, returned to their former retreat. More depredations followed. After several narrow escapes Philip, who had received his American name from the magistrates at Plymouth, was tracked to Mount Hope (now the beautiful property of R. F. Haffenreffer, near Bristol, Rhode Island), and was killed by an Indian whose brother had been put to death by Philip for advising that peace be made. On this spot is a memorial stone and tablet rather difficult to find without a guide.

MASONIC

IT WAS in the McGilvary yard at Stockton (now Stockton Springs), Waldo County, Maine, that this barque, launched on July 19, 1864, was constructed by Albion P. Goodhue, master builder, for Henry S. Staples of the firm of Staples & Triffin. (The official slogan of Stockton Springs, by the way, is "The Little Town with Big Possibilities.") Later owners of the "Masonic" were Birch & Lord, Noah Emery and H. P. Blanchard. Her registration was changed to New York in 1880 and last appears on the list of American Merchant ships for 1885.

Henry W. Peabody of Boston was her agent on the voyage to Melbourne, Australia, advertised by the accompanying card. Even though a date is given on the card (not the date of sailing, however) we regret that we found it impossible to learn any further details about her career in addition to the bare information presented above.

It seems safe to assume that one or more of her original owners were members of the fraternity whose name was carried by this vessel but we found no records to prove it.

The "Steam Job Printer" on the bottom of this card aroused our interest and after several inquiries we learned from Mr. William E. Crosby, Secretary of the Ancient and Honorable Artillery Company, who in addition to being a well known printer in Boston is quite an historian as well, that when printers first put in steam-powered presses it was considered quite an advance in their art, so they generally added the words "Steam Job Printer" to their names to indicate their enterprise and progressiveness.

FOR MELBOURNE.

From Commercial Wharf.

The A 1 Fast Sailing Barque

MASONIC

ONLY 540 TONS REGISTER.

I. LANPHER, ... *Commander.*

Will be promptly despatched as above, having a large portion of her cargo ready to go on board,

Sailing day will shortly be advertised,

And strictly conformed to, as usual.

For Freight or Cabin Passage, apply to

HENRY W. PEABODY,

BOSTON, Dec. 12, 1867.   11 LIBERTY SQUARE,

Messrs. NEWELL & CO., Commission Merchants. Consignees at Melbourne.

Fred Rogers, Steam Job Printer, 139 Washington Street, Boston.

Courtesy of Bostonian Society

NEPTUNE'S FAVORITE

THERE IS NOTHING particularly exciting to report concerning this "Extreme A 1 Clipper Ship" which travelled the seas for over twenty years, finally hailing from Glasgow in 1874. London seems to have been frequently her port of call and her cargoes appear to have consisted chiefly of tea or guano — two quite different substances! She was particularly popular in England. Her owners spared no pains in advertising her as a "magnificent ship, has no superior, and scarcely a rival in the trade. In model, build, ventilation and all appointments, she is truly superb" . . . "*always* makes quick time, and delivers her cargo in superior condition. We request shippers to visit her and think they will readily agree with us, that she is *The Ship of the Port*, and by *far* the most desirable conveyance now offering for San Francisco."

She was built by Jotham Stetson at Chelsea in 1854 for H. A. Kelly & Co. of Boston. Stetson at one time had his yard on South Street, just above Winthrop Street Bridge in Medford, Mass., where he built 32 vessels. "Neptune's Favorite" was sold in 1865 at London for £800, the highest price ever paid during that period for any vessel of her size, and was then renamed "Mataura," hailing from Glasgow. Her various commanders were Oliver G. Lane, Emmerton, Stewart and Watts. This vessel should not be confused with "Neptune's Car," upon which an unusual episode in the annals of the sea took place. Young Captain Potter in his 29th year was taken ill with brain fever and entirely incapacitated even to assist in navigation; also, the first mate was under arrest for insubordination. The Captain's young wife, only nineteen years old but fortunately an expert in seamanship, brought the "Car" to port in addition to nursing her sick husband, a story with "no parallel in fiction," according to writers. Mrs. Potter has been referred to as the "Florence Nightingale of the Ocean."

Courtesy of Peabody Museum

OCEAN EXPRESS

THIS VESSEL was another Medford product, the builder being J. O. Curtis, who also built the "Eagle Wing" already mentioned in this brochure. It is said the "Ocean Express" was the largest ship ever turned out at Medford. In spite of the builder's prophecy that she would be "First in speed, first in beauty and first in the world of waters," she met with a great deal of misfortune and cost the insurance companies large sums of money. Notwithstanding her many mishaps, mostly due to sprung timbers, she plowed many seas from 1854 to 1890, and among her far-flung places of call were Peru, San Salvador, Bahia, Montevideo, Callao, Puget Sound and Costa Rica. During the Civil War she was used by the United States Army as a transport, and at one time she flew the German flag and later the Norwegian colors. While under the American flag she was the property of Reed, Wade & Co. and their successors Samuel G. Reed & Co. of Boston. The former firm had offices at 16 North Market Street in 1854 and the partners were Samuel G. Reed, whose home was at 3 Allen Street, Boston, and Reuben S. Wade, who lived in Charlestown. Around 1858, Wade apparently retired from the firm and the name was changed to Samuel G. Reed & Co., with offices at 85 State Street, Boston.

While at Liverpool in 1855 ready to sail for New York, the crew of the "Ocean Express" mutinied and were landed on English soil, stranded and without sufficient clothes. The American Consul, however, had the duty of providing for their welfare.

Her many commanders doubtless have numerous descendants scattered over New England and elsewhere. Their names were Cunningham, Hutchinson, Hotchkiss, Willis, Hale, Watson, Cushing, Warsaw, and Horton.

Courtesy of American Antiquarian Society

ONWARD

THE CLIPPER Barque "Onward" of the Hawaiian Packet Line was advertised by Charles W. Brooks & Co. to sail for Honolulu from San Francisco. This same firm was one of the references used by C. Brewer & Company in an announcement made in 1859. Other interesting facts connecting Honolulu with our shipping cards appear in the history of the Brewer firm which mentions that Peter C. Jones, a partner, sailed to Honolulu in the "John Gilpin"; that another, John D. Brewer, took the "Syren" to the Islands, and a third partner, Thomas D. Hinckley, owned an interest in the "Don Quixote," all three names being shown on sailing cards included in this booklet, though, as will be noted later in this chapter, the "Don Quixote" card we have used refers to another vessel of the same name.

Honolulu was very familiar to vessels from the U. S. A.; for whalers and clippers, as shown in the accompanying photograph, frequently called at the Islands for repairs and provisions. For

Courtesy Charles Brewer   *From "A History of C. Brewer & Company, Ltd., 1826–1926"*
by Josephine Sullivan

PORT OF HONOLULU IN 1857

these reasons we have added here a short history of the Brewer firm, still a very influential house there and for some time well known here when members of the Brewer family, E. M. Brewer and Joseph Brewer, acted as agents in Boston. This firm, later to be incorporated, celebrated the one-hundredth year of its existence in 1926 and the story of its interesting career was loaned to us by Charles Brewer, President of the Warren Institution for Savings, Boston, a grandson of Captain Charles Brewer. The firm was started by James Hunnewell, grandfather of James M. Hunnewell, prominent lawyer of Boston, who left Boston for Honolulu in 1817. From a sailor he rose to be an officer and in 1826 he returned to the Islands as first mate of the "Thaddeus" which brought the first missionaries to Hawaii. As he had become familiar with conditions there, he started in business for himself. He had with him on board this so-called "Missionary Ship" a small cargo of merchandise, with which he started the firm which eventually increased greatly in size, owning at least thirteen plantations. Hunnewell soon took in as associate Henry A. Peirce, also of Boston. When the former retired to Charlestown, the latter became the head of the firm, which continued to prosper. Thomas D. Hinckley became a partner under the name of Peirce & Hinckley. The latter's contribution to the organization was a one-quarter interest in the earlier vessel named "Don Quixote." The card we have reproduced announces the sailing of the second vessel of the same name.

To Captain Charles Brewer of Boston came the distinction of renaming and extending the business after navigating vessels to a number of foreign ports, settling at Honolulu in 1836. The concern was then called Peirce & Brewer, and a few years later C. Brewer & Co. A nephew of Captain Brewer, by name Charles Brewer, 2nd, came to the Islands and became a partner about 1845. At that time a great variety of articles were dealt in — silks, beaver hats, hides, teas, iron hoops, hardware, navy soap, saddles, crockery, glassware, molasses, lumber and, of course, sugar. A newspaper in Honolulu printed in 1861 a flattering anonymous article about him, ending with the statement that "Brewer, taken as a man, is about as good as they make them nowadays." After the Civil War the firm became agents for a fleet of five vessels, one of which was called "John D. Brewer." The discovery of gold changed the situation and the merchants in the Islands turned their attention to sending a variety of articles to San Francisco that had to do with mining. Brewer & Co. first became interested in the sandalwood trade, then followed the trade in sperm oil and whalebone brought there by the many whalers. Later sugar became the leading business of the firm, and the dealings in that article were carried on with America, China and Australia. Charles Brewer 2nd himself visited the gold fields, but his stay there was only a brief one.

In 1859 the company advertised itself as "Ship Agents and General Commission Merchants," and in fact as the notice read "all other business appertaining to shipping," and "also the sales of merchandise generally." Henry A. P. Carter, whose parents lived in Charlestown, became a partner in 1862, and his son, George Robert, served from 1903 to 1907 as the second Governor of the Islands.

Peter C. Jones of Boston became manager of the firm about 1857. As already noted, he made the journey in the "John Gilpin" commanded by Captain Ropes, which vessel, it would seem, was active in carrying out to Honolulu several men destined to become members of C. Brewer & Co. Jones tells upon arrival of passing the "Boston Building" and noticing the sign over the door "Charles Brewer, 2nd." Nearby he met a man who remarked, "Another fellow has come from Boston; we had better make up a purse of $10,000 and send him right home." Jones declared to himself he would have compromised for half that sum. It was Carter who made the remark, and it is interesting to note that it wasn't long before Carter and Jones became partners, continuing as such for twenty years.

QUICK DISPATCH! FIRST CLASS CLIPPERS!

HAWAIIAN PACKET LINE

FOR

HONOLULU, H. I.

The First Class A 1 Extreme Clipper Barque

450 TONS. DENISON HEMPSTEAD, Commander,

Is receiving cargo at CLAY STREET WHARF, and will have immediate dispatch. Insures at Lowest Rates. Vessels of this Line have superior Cabin and Steerage accommodations, fitted expressly for comfort and convenience of Passengers. Engagements made at lowest current rates.

For Terms, Apply to

Agents at Honolulu, **CHAS. W. BROOKS & CO.**

Messrs. ALDRICH, WALKER & CO. **511 Sansome Street, cor. of Merchant.**

Wm. P. Harrison & Co's Print, 417 Clay Street, San Francisco.

Courtesy of American Antiquarian Society

The firm became incorporated in 1883 and among the assets were the Hawaiian Agricultural Company, Wailuku Sugar Company, Onomea Sugar Company, and Honomu Sugar Company. A statement recently received from the Hawaiian Economic Foundation lists C. Brewer & Co. Ltd. as having assets of $17,365,787.

The "Onward" was another of the ships built by J. O. Curtis at Medford for Reed, Wade & Co. of Boston. The Goddess of Liberty served as her figurehead while an American Indian adorned the stern. Captain Jesse G. Cotting superintended her construction and became her first commander, being succeeded by Thomas F. Wade, followed by Captain E. A. Luce. In 1861 she became a Government cruiser and was equipped with guns. During the Civil War she cruised for Confederate privateers and on the termination of hostilities she was used by the Navy for a storeship. She continued her usefulness for a number of years and was sold in 1884 for $1,850.

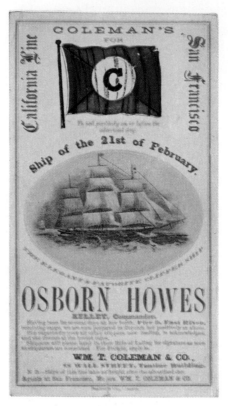

Courtesy of Peabody Museum

OSBORN HOWES

THE MEMBERS of the Howes family were typical Cape Codders, for the earliest arrival came to Dennis, Massachusetts as early as 1635. The father of Osborn Howes was a sea captain and while serving in the War of 1812 was captured, but recaptured his vessel and sailed it into Portland Harbor. The son for whom this ship was named was born in Dennis in 1806, the second of five children. His autobiography, or sketch, as he calls it, is in possession of his great-grandson, who is now in the employ of the

State Street Trust Company, and gives an interesting description of the routine life of the family during his boyhood in Dennis. He writes that economy was very necessary, and all of the clothing for the household was of his mother's production; that during the winter months spinning-wheels were put in motion for flax, cotton and wool, and also looms for weaving very durable cloth; then the cow had to be milked, the pig fed, and water brought from the spring some distance away, and the children had to be cared for.

Changing one's residence was a difficult undertaking in those days. In 1818 the family moved from Dennis to Dedham, by schooner to Boston, and thence by stage coach. Young Howes journeyed with the furniture by ox team and his record of the trip explains that he "sat on the frame of a bedstead which projected out from the hinder part of the wagon."

Osborn Howes first went to sea as supercargo, but rose to be captain of vessels, making voyages to Copenhagen, Brazil, Pernambuco and Turkey. He later entered business in Boston in partnership with his brother-in-law, Nathan Crowell, under the name of Howes & Crowell. This partnership, well known at the time, continued for thirty-four years, and managed or owned many merchant ships. The firm transacted business with China, Australia, the East Indies and Western Europe, as well as with California and South America. From small beginnings their business expanded and prospered, especially during the twenty years following the discovery of gold in California. Howes' diary lists the names of forty-three vessels (including the ship "Osborn Howes") which he owned in whole or in part or managed during his business career. He was the father of nine children, and lived to the ripe old age of eighty-seven years. At his death a friend wrote of him: "He was to me a type of the New Englander which is not passing away but passing on into a series of different types. To have had personal acquaintance with him was to believe forever in the men who made us a nation and consequently to have faith in its future."

A good deal of space has been given to the man for whom this ship was named for the reason that the ship itself met with no particular adventure except for the loss of an entire set of sails while fighting gales for twenty-five days in rounding Cape Horn. She was called a "good sailer" by her first captain, Nehemiah Kelley of Brewster. In 1864 she was at Calcutta to go under the British flag. This sailing card is not colorful but is included as it was named for a distinguished personage whose descendants are many.

★　　★　　★

SANCHO PANZA

JOHN ELLERTON LODGE of Boston, must have been an admirer of the writings of that famous Spanish author, Cervantes, as he named two of his ships after leading characters in "Don Quixote" — one for the hero and the other for the latter's faithful but dumb squire, Sancho Panza. Both of these clippers are among those mentioned in this volume.

The picture on the accompanying card is based on the illustration in "Don Quixote" showing Sancho being tossed in a blanket by some mischievous fellow-guests at the little inn where he and his master had stopped after one of their many adventures. (The ship in the background was added by the illustrator of the card as it does not appear in the original.) Sancho's hazing came when he was not quick enough in getting away with Don Quixote when the latter dashed off on his gallant steed Rozinante, after telling the innkeeper that it was against the laws of knight-errantry and beneath his rank and dignity to pay the expenses of lodging and feeding himself and his attendant, with their mounts, at the hostelry. Sancho's mount, by the way, was a lowly donkey, shown in the illustration.

FOR
SANFRANCISCO
Guaranteed for June 6th.

THE A 1 EXTREME CLIPPER SHIP

SANCHO PANZA

ELIAS DAVIS, Master,

IS NOW READY FOR CARGO, AT PIER 15 E. R.

Her small capacity, unsurpassed sailing qualities, and the quick dispatch she will have, render her the most desirable vessel on the berth.

Freight can now be engaged at favorable rates, on application to

BINGHAM & REYNOLDS, 88 Wall Street.

NESBITT & CO., PRINTERS.

*Courtesy of Alfred Mansfield of the Cape Ann Scientific, Literary
and Historical Society, Gloucester, Mass.*

The clipper "Sancho Panza" was built at Medford in 1855 by Samuel Lapham and at the end of her maiden voyage from Boston to San Francisco, which took 147 days, her Captain, John B. Hildreth, was so disgusted that he wrote in her log "The devil take Sancho Panza, she is as bad as her namesake." However, one expert who studied the log put the blame on the commander instead of the ship, concluding that she had not been properly handled. Before completing this initial trip, she went from San Francisco to Foo Chow, China, and loaded for Boston. She last sailed under the American flag from New York to Melbourne, thence to Singapore, Shanghai, Hong Kong, Foo Chow and London. This voyage lasted from July 13, 1861 until January 3, 1863. Her Captain, Nathaniel Hale, who had been in command of her for several years, died in London three days after her arrival, at the age of 43. She was then sold to the British and her name changed to "Nimrod." She continued under that name when sold to German interests around 1890. Described as a "very neat and pretty little ship," the "Sancho Panza," quite fittingly, seemed to have done a lot of wandering in her career as did the character after which she was named. In her peregrinations, she visited Hong Kong, Shanghai and Foo Chow several times and also touched at Woosung, China, and Anjer, Java, at least twice while under American ownership.

SEAMAN'S BRIDE

THIS MEDIUM CLIPPER, shown by the card as under the management of the well known firm of Nathaniel Winsor & Co. of Boston, was built at Belfast, Waldo County, Maine, by Carter & Co. in 1856 for Enoch Benner, Daniel Lewis and others of Boston. The city directory of that year shows that Benner was a partner in the firm of Benner & Kilborn, West India goods and shipchandlers, of 178 Commercial Street and 155 Fulton Street, Boston. Daniel Lewis is listed as a commission merchant with place of business at 99 State Street. Benner's home was in Chelsea and Lewis lived in Roxbury.

We regret that in spite of a great deal of research we were unable to discover any further reference to the "Seaman's Bride" except that she was lost in 1865 at Baker's Island in the Pacific, a fate of which the sad-eyed female on the card we have reproduced seems to have had a premonition. Octavius Thorndike Howe stated that of the 231 clippers of which there are records 45 foundered at sea or were never heard from.

In our search for information we ran across the fact that there was another "Seaman's Bride" — one of the celebrated Baltimore clippers built by R. and E. Bell in 1851, of the same model and slightly smaller than their clipper "Seaman" produced the year before in the same yard. This "Seaman's Bride" made several voyages under New York owners and was sold in 1855 to merchants of Hamburg, Germany, after a voyage there from New York which lasted 26 days. Her new owners changed her name to "Carl Staegoman." It was the next year that the Maine "Seaman's Bride" was built and the name once more took its place on the list of American ships.

The "Seaman's Bride" of Baltimore was more fortunate than the "Seaman," which was struck by lightning and burned to the water's edge on February 6, 1855 while bound from New Orleans to Marseilles, so it might be said the "Seaman's Bride" was widowed early in 1855 and later that year changed her name.

Courtesy of American Antiquarian Society

SPITFIRE

THIS NAME became familiar throughout the world during World War II when we all followed with the greatest eagerness news of the exploits of those fast fighting ships of the air which did such outstanding and effective work in the defense of Britain. Built by Vickers Armstrongs, Ltd., they were appropriately named, as the definition of the word is given in the dictionaries as "a violent, irascible person" and they certainly proved to be that to the Germans. By coincidence, the clipper "Spitfire," which was built by James Arey & Co., of Frankfort, Maine, for Thomas Gray and Manning & Stanwood of Boston, was sold to the British in 1863. Perhaps it is too much to expect that the fighting plane of recent years was named for this early clipper. The name seems to connote speed as the clipper "Spitfire," described on the accompanying card as "one of the fastest of the clipper fleet," was said never to have been beaten in a race by any loaded ship except the "Witchcraft." While under command of Captain Samuel R. Leach, she sailed a dead heat race to San Francisco with the "Black Hawk" (also mentioned in this volume) commanded by Captain B. P. Bowers. The "Spitfire" left Boston on December 21st, 1860, and the "Black Hawk" passed Sandy Hook the same day. Both ships arrived at San Francisco on the 8th of April of the following year — a passage of 107 days. It might be interesting to mention that in those days the rare passages around the Horn of less than 100 days were generally referred to as "around the Horn in two figures." On her maiden voyage to San Francisco from Boston the "Spitfire" was under command of the hard-driving Captain John Arey in the China-London tea trade. Arey, it was said, expected his men to be able to "jump over the fore-yard before breakfast." This statement was also attributed to her chief mate, Elkanah Crowell, later Captain of the "Boston Light," when eight men

100 DAYS TO SAN FRANCISCO. COLEMAN'S California Line FOR SAN FRANCISCO

IMMEDIATE DISPATCH.

FIRST-CLASS CLIPPERS.

The A 1 Extreme Clipper Ship

"SPITFIRE,"

SAM'L K. LEACH, Commander, is now rapidly Loading at Pier 15 East River, foot Wall Street.

This superb vessel is unsurpassed in every requisite for Strength, Speed and Ventilation. She has made three passages to San Francisco in 100, 118 and 107 days respectively, always delivering her cargo in fine order. She insures at lowest rates, and has a large portion of her cargo engaged. For balance of freight, apply to

WM. T. COLEMAN & CO., 88 Wall St., Tontine Building.

Agents in San Francisco, Messrs. WM. T. COLEMAN & CO.

Exchange on San Francisco for sale in sums to suit. Advances made on shipments of Approved Merchandise.

SHARPS & SON. PRINTERS.

Courtesy of Peabody Museum

of the crew had to be discharged at Rio for incompetence on this initial voyage which ran into bad weather causing damage enough to have her put into Rio for repairs. Apparently he did not consider these eight men capable of performing this early morning feat! The "Spitfire" was said to be one of the most beautiful of the clipper fleet as well as one of the fastest. She was seen in many foreign ports, including Callao, Honolulu, Hong Kong, Foo Chow, Queenstown, Liverpool and Hull before she arrived in London on April of 1863 in damaged condition. She was then sold to the British, as stated above, and her new owners continued to operate her under the same name.

Partners of Manning & Stanwood, who shared in her ownership when constructed, were Francis C. Manning, E. C. Stanwood and R. W. Lord, with headquarters at 15 Central Wharf, Boston.

From the collection of the State Street Trust Company

SYREN

THE "SYREN" suffered more accidents than almost any other vessel, without actually sinking. Nevertheless she had the distinction of surviving longer than any other of the clipper fleet, as she was listed in Lloyd's as late as 1920 under the changed name of "Margarida" of Buenos Aires. Her misfortunes on her voyages to San Francisco were too numerous to mention except in a general way. On the passage from Honolulu to New Bedford, her bow was twisted, and everything on deck, including all the boats, skylights, etc., was washed overboard. The wheel was also split. In addition to this damage she was struck by lightning and lost two of her crew overboard. On the return journey she again had her bow stove in. As she was beating out of San Francisco, she lost steerage way and struck a rock, receiving further damage. For a second time she grounded and returned to the harbor with four feet of water in her hold, was beached and obliged to discharge her cargo which was badly soaked. On later voyages she lost jib boom, sails and topmasts. Returning to Boston she met with a collision, but fortunately escaped with only slight damage. As late as 1888, misfortune still was following her, for on a voyage to California she was obliged to put into Rio leaking badly, where she was repaired.

The "Syren" was launched in 1851 by John Taylor at Medford. At first she had a siren for a figurehead which perhaps was considered unlucky for her, so this was changed to an eagle's head. Silsbee & Pickman ordered her building and towards the end of the 1850s she became Boston owned, by Joseph Hunnewell. On her maiden voyage in 1851 she left Boston under command of Captain Edward A. Silsbee.

A particularly interesting fact is that her next owner was Charles Brewer & Co. of Honolulu, concerning which firm we have a good deal to say under another heading. Her final ownership rested in a citizen of New Bedford, William H. Besse.

THATCHER MAGOUN

THERE IS a beautiful model of the "Thatcher Magoun" in the Marine Room of Phillips Academy at Andover, a gift of Moreau Delano, a great-grandson of the shipbuilder for whom the vessel was named. This medium clipper was built by Hayden & Cudworth at Medford for the Magoun firm, composed of father and son, and curiously enough the builder of the model was the expert craftsman Bernard Hart whose home was in Malden, which adjoins Medford. Many of his models adorn the houses of New England ship-lovers. The clipper's first voyage was from Boston to San Francisco under Captain Sylvannus Bourne. On a voyage fourteen years later, under the same Captain Peterson of Duxbury whose name appears on the accompanying card and who made nineteen voyages in her, the Boston vessel sighted the French brig "Grand Frederic" of Rochelle lying unmanageable on her broadside. The entire crew of the unfortunate vessel was saved, the Captain and officers of the "Magoun" later receiving medals from the French Government. A painting of this rescue by J. Hughes of Liverpool is in the Andover Marine Gallery.

A most complete story of this vessel, and of the Thatcher Magoun for whom she was named and the son of the same name, was compiled by Hollis French in 1934. From his quotation from the log of the "Thatcher Magoun" (incorrectly spelled on the card we have reproduced) we found that the date of the sailing advertised on the card was May 25, 1867. The last entry, on July 29, reads "Damn the Straits." He wrote of this vessel's uncertain end: "Perhaps it is as well to leave her fate shrouded in mystery, for it would be sad to think of the end of a once proud and noble vessel which had so long sailed the seven seas." Hall Gleason, the Medford historian, wrote that this vessel was sold to Norwegians, renamed the "Hercules" and was reported lost off the coast of Africa in the early '80s. A bronze image of Magoun served as a figurehead.

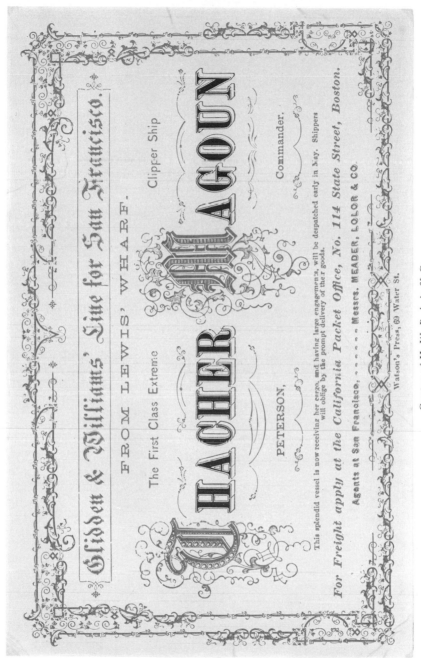

Glidden & Williams' Line for San Francisco.

FROM LEWIS' WHARF.

The First Class Extreme Clipper Ship

J. HACHER LAGOUN

PETERSON, Commander.

This splendid vessel is now receiving her cargo, and having large engagements, will be despatched early in May. Shippers will oblige by the prompt delivery of their goods.

For Freight apply at the California Packet Office, No. 114 State Street, Boston.

Agents at San Francisco, ------ Messrs. MEADER, LOLOR & CO.

Watson's Press, 69 Water St.

The elder Magoun, who was born in Pembroke on the day the Battle of Bunker Hill was fought, was known as the father of shipbuilding on the Mystic River. He worked five years in Salem at the shipyard of Enos Briggs. He also worked in Charlestown for a while and then selected the shores of the Mystic River for his yard. Although offered assistance in getting established there, he politely refused it, saying that he could not afford to be helped. Here his vessels were constructed on Riverside Avenue, south of Park Street. His residence was near by on Ship Street or Park Street, and later on High Street, now the Medford Library. He took his son into partnership in 1856, the year of his death, and the year of the launching of the "Magoun." The office was then located at 66 State Street, Boston. In 1936 his descendants placed a bronze plaque on the site of his counting house on State Street, now numbered 70.

The Magoun firm ranks in importance in volume of production with Donald McKay of East Boston, for the former constructed before 1836 at least eighty of the five hundred and sixty-seven ships launched along the Mystic, and eleven more were built between 1836 and 1856.

A niece of the wife of the elder Thatcher wrote interestingly of the shipyard and mansion house:

"I grew familiar with every nook and corner of this old house on Ship Street.

Do you recall the Square in Medford? If you should walk from there easterly, you would enter Ship Street, and pass by on the left the old graveyard and the brick building, now black with age, where for many years Medford rum — famous all over the world for its excellent quality — was made. You would go past pleasant pastures, over a little stream on a small bridge, known as Gravelly Bridge. . . . At some distance in front of-the house flows the pretty Mystic River. On its banks stands the Medford Shipyard, including the shiphouse, one hundred feet high, the workhouse and the blacksmith's shop. Go down where you see the busy workmen. The master is walking leisurely around, giving his directions. It is interesting to climb the long flight of steps and look down into the two big ships in the process of building. Still more so would it be to see them glide gracefully into the water at the time of launching."

COLEMAN'S

FOR

California Line — TO SAIL POSITIVELY — 1st to 5th DECEMBER. — **San Francisco.**

SHIP OF 29TH NOVEMBER.

THE EXTREMELY BEAUTIFUL

CLIPPER SHIP

WESTWARD HO!

HUSSEY, Commander,

IS NOW RECEIVING CARGO AT PIER 9, EAST RIVER.

This is THE Clipper of the Port. Undoubtedly *the fastest* Ship now up. She has made the three best voyages to San Francisco of any ship afloat, having accomplished the same in 105, 97 and 100 days respectively.

Her thorough ventilation, and the admirable manner in which she has always delivered her cargo, render her the most desirable vessel now loading. SHE INSURES AT LOWEST RATES. For Freight, apply to

WILLIAM T. COLEMAN & CO.,

88 WALL ST., Tontine Building.

Courtesy of Clark Collection, Francis Russell Hart Nautical Museum, Massachusetts Institute of Technology

WESTWARD HO

THE NAME "WESTWARD HO" affords an opportunity to mention very briefly some of the vessels and companies that sailed from Massachusetts to California one hundred years ago, together with some of their experiences. The total number of ships sailing from this State was two hundred and fifty, one hundred and fifty-one from Boston, forty-two from New Bedford, eight from Nantucket, six from Newburyport, six from Gloucester and the rest from other ports. The first vessel to depart from Boston with an organized company was the Boston & California Joint Stock Mining & Trading Company in the "Edward Everett," named for the then President of Harvard College who gave a hundred volumes to the ship's library with the instructions to "take the Bible in one hand and your New England civilization in the other." The members met in late December of 1848 at the Hanover House in Boston and upon arrival in San Francisco erected a building which they gave the same name. One of the passengers on the "Everett" wrote home, describing the rations: "We live very well, better than I expected. We get our grub in a kid and sit down on the deck, ten men to a mess, and eat it right out of the tub. We have dandy funk, made of hard bread boiled with molasses, raisins and cinnamon, apple grunt made by stewing dried apples and dough balls. Lobscouse made by hashing up meat and bread and heating. We have duff, flour pudding, etc." They also laid out streets and localities which they called Beacon Street, Dock Square and North End. Other groups to get away early were the Boston & Newburyport Mining Company, the Massasoit Company from Lowell, another group from Holyoke, which found at a camp on the Panama route "samples of all the abominable reptiles which these poisonous regions afford."

The Beverly Joint Stock San Francisco Company marched down Cabot Street of that Massachusetts city in August of 1849 and on the voyage one of their number composed a song to the tune of "Susannah, Don't You Cry." Several lines were:

"We started from 'Old Beverly,'
Mid cheers from great and small.
We hope to get back bye and bye,
    When we'll return them all,

The fair sex wept, the boys hurrahed,
And we'd no time to cry.

We doubled close 'round Beverly bar,
'Twas close upon our lee,
We then hove to and called the roll,
And squared away for sea.

Now here's success, you'll surely say,
To all you willing souls
And may you have the joyful chance,
Of filling all your bowls.
But not just yet, but by and by,
And full of glittering ore,
And then return to where you wish
And never want for more.

We'll see you bye and bye,
If we've good luck, and if we don't
Why bless you, don't you cry."

A member of the company kept a journal of this voyage and on August 18 the Melodeon Band gave a concert, followed soon afterwards by the death of a pet crow which was much missed although he was a "thieving blackguard." Things began then to go wrong, the dog got cross, water leaked into the berths and ran into the cabin, causing one of the voyagers to write these amusing few lines:

"A smoky house, a scolding wife,
Are miseries of human life —
A leaky ship in squally weather,
Is worse than both of these together."

There was another Beverly company called The Bay State & California Mining & Trading Company, composed of twenty-nine residents of that North Shore city, which left from Boston. One member brought out a supply of gold and silver watches purchased at Bigelow & Kennard's, but no one took any interest in the silver ones, gold being in the minds of every one. Another explorer wrote home, "I wonder that I was ever discontented in Boston."

A Boston & Newton Company took the difficult all land route and fared better than most. There was also a large Boston & New England Company, several of the members being left behind as the "Leonore" departed from the wharf in Boston. There were several other groups with "Massachusetts" in their names. A so-called Cochituate Trading & Mining Company was composed of sixty men from towns in Essex County and Cape Cod, commanded by John Dillingham, a well known resident of Brewster. Their conveyance sailed from Fisk's Wharf in Boston.

Two companies of the same name, Bunker Hill, went on the same ship, spending forty days almost in sight of Cape Horn. Much was said about the "Horn" and one stanza we quote from "American Sea Songs & Chanteys, From the Days of Iron Men and Wooden Ships," Edited by Frank Shay, Illustrated by Edward A. Wilson, W. W. Norton & Co. Inc., 1948.

> "I wish to God I'd never been born
>   To me way, hay, o-hio!
> To drag my carcass around Cape Horn
>   A long time ago!"

Cape Ann contributed to the list of Argonauts, one company from Essex, Manchester, Rockport and Gloucester departing in a schooner named "Boston." A Hampden group were so seasick that they said they would prefer to go overland on their hands and knees rather than experience another ocean voyage. A member of the Middlesex & California Gold Company became so homesick that he entered in the log of the "Sea Eagle," — "I assure you old South Reading with its pretty houses, green fields, pies and beans looked good to me."

On the ship "Capitol" owned by Sampson & Tappan went the Naumkeag Company, of Salem of course, from Lewis Wharf in Boston. She was advertised to have better food and better quarters than other vessels, but the passengers were soon complaining about their conditions, even threatening mutiny. At Rio, however, they made up for their disappointments on the voyage by sightseeing and by attending horse races, cock fights and dances. This group originated a song to the tune of the "Old Oaken Bucket" (substituting the word "leather" for "oaken"), inspired by the action of one of the crew who set adrift the bucket which had drawn up the water from which every one washed. The stanzas may be read in the "Argonauts of '49" by Howe.

The North Western Company was a cooperative group which proposed to make its money by trading instead of mining. Their conveyance, the "Orb," encountered bad weather and water ran into the staterooms. Upon reaching Sacramento she was turned into a store ship and each one went "on his own."

Some Harvard students known as the Old Harvard Company were recruited to sail on the "Duxbury" along with another unnamed company. One of the latter was followed down to the wharf by the sheriff. Time for their departure was approaching and something had to be done. He saw a grocery store near by and the manager shoved him into a box, which he marked "Medicine — This side up — Handle with care." It was said that, by mischance, the fugitive for some time had to remain up side down. Near San Francisco was a locality known as Happy Valley and there the Harvard Company set up a tent and from it was flown a flag with the name of the organization "Old Harvard Company, Cambridge" on it.

The yards of New Bedford and Nantucket converted whalers for the California voyage until it was said that it looked as if at the next election in Nantucket there would scarcely be anyone left to vote. The well known Coffin family, as one might expect, fitted out the first vessel to sail from the island seaport. The first group to leave New Bedford was the New Bedford & California Mining Company on another "Mayflower."

The Congress & California Mutual Protection Association, composed of fifty young men from Roxbury, was organized as a military body and their mistake was to take too much baggage, along with wagons and provisions, necessitating the abandonment of wagons, some of which they broke up and used as fuel to cook their meals.

The Sagamore & Sacramento Company of Lynn, consisting of fifty-two men, marched down State Street with their flags flying, accompanied by a band of music and doubtless much cheering. They wore uniforms and their wagons and harnesses were made to order. They had four men and four horses for each vehicle. Upon their arrival in New York they held another dress parade.

The Sandwich & Cape Cod Mining & Trading Company which took the Panama route held, on the island of Tobago, a celebration of the landing of the Pilgrims which was shared in by all the ships in the harbor.

A Salem company known later as the La Grange Company was named for the vessel upon which it sailed. From this group later originated the "Society of California Pioneers of New England." As was often the custom, when there was an important sailing from Salem, a song was sung just before the ship left her berth and several stanzas are copied here:

> "Oh! the gold is there, most anywhere
> And they dig it out with an iron bar,
> And when it's thick, with a spade and pick,
> They've taken out lumps as big as a brick.
>
> In the days of old, the Prophets told
> Of the City to come, all framed in gold,
> Peradventure they foresaw the day,
> Now dawning in California."

The journal of this voyage mentions that a man and three hens went overboard but that all were rescued. The narrator of the event stated that hens would bring $25 apiece in California, but no mention is made of the value of a human life.

The ship "Sweden" in early March took out the Mt. Washington Company and the Roxbury Sagamore Company and a group of twenty-five Cambridge men. On the Sunday before sailing this group of pioneers attended services in Father Taylor's Seamen's Bethel in North Square in Boston. This well known preacher undoubtedly gave the congregation one of his sermons flavored with nautical expressions, as was frequently his custom. A story of this original minister is included in one of the Trust Company's booklets entitled "Old Shipping Days in Boston," now out of print.

In 1850 Captain Octavius T. Howe caught the gold fever and fitted out the "Tigress," previously owned by David Pingree and George West, loading her with every kind of odds and ends from the Beverly and Salem shops. She became a veritable department store, and, according to the California papers, Howe lost money on the shipment.

Many other organized companies are described in Howe's "Argonauts of '49." This author mentions those that preferred the Cape Horn all sea route, those who went across the Isthmus of Panama, those who crossed via Mexico and some who took the land route and suffered very severely. The men who went by water seemed to arrive in better condition to do the work at the mines than any of the others. One company to go by land declared that the mosquitoes were so thick in one place that if you elevated your hat on a stick and removed the latter, the hat would still be buoyed up in the air by the mosquitoes.

An adventurer about to depart from the mine fields wrote:

"I'm bound from California, I'm homeward bound once more,
I'm leaving fast this humbug land, with all its glittering ore.
I've travelled far o'er hill and dale, gained bruises and hard knocks,
And now am leaving satisfied with a pocket full of rocks."

Another described his experiences in a similar vein:

"But I'm bound off, I've got my load, my shovel I've laid down,
  My pick and crow and pan and spoon, I've left upon the ground,
  My cradle I can rock at home, if ever there I get,
  And there I'm bound with empty purse and pockets all to let."

Many made the remark that "Spades were trumps" in California. Most of the companies disbanded at Sacramento, which was nicknamed the "Powder Magazine" because so many blew up there.

From late in 1848, the year of the California gold discovery, through the year 1849, practically every day the newspapers of Boston carried news items and reports from the Golden State, telling of the experiences of adventurers there. "California News," "More California Stories," "Letter from the Mines," "Rapine and Murder in California" were typical headings of the stories which appeared so frequently.

An instance indicating how the California gold craze pervaded the thinking of the times, is the naming of a local episode that occurred in 1849, "The Expedition of the Cape Cod & Charlestown Gold Mining Company." According to Donald G. Trayser, Clerk of the Courts, Barnstable, Mass., in his interesting column "Once Upon a Time on Cape Cod," which is a regular feature of the "*Cape Codder*" published by Jack Johnson of Orleans, Mass., one of the most fantastic escapes from the State Prison at Charlestown, Mass., took place on May 14, 1849. A resourceful convict, imprisoned for robbery, confided to the Warden that he had buried the $50,000 stolen from a Wheeling, West Virginia, bank in a secluded spot on Cape Cod and offered to lead him to the treasure. The Warden believed him and, with an assistant, set out with the prisoner to recover the loot. He led them to a spot in Cotuit near the Osterville line and they started digging. As the hole grew deeper, they took turns in shovelling. While one of the officers of the law was in the hole digging, the prisoner pushed the other into the pit and dashed away. Being the year of the gold rush, it was quite natural that the Boston newspapers gave it the amusing label by which it became known. Incidentally, the escaped prisoner was recaptured three months later and safely jailed for the rest of his prison sentence, bearing out the old precept that crime does not pay!

As has been stated in our Foreword, not all the fortunes were made from the gold found in California, as is indicated by the following advertisement in the *Boston Evening Traveller* of January 31, 1849:

> "CALIFORNIA GOODS
>
> G. C. Holman, 15 & 17 Kilby Street, invites attention to his large assortment of Fancy and Staple Goods, adapted to the California and Pacific Trade, on which Shippers and Adventurers will be sure *to realize handsome profits*. The assortment embraces Beads, Jewelry, Mirrors, Soap, Colognes, Brushes, Combs, Cutlery, Purses, Cigar Cases, Tobacco and Snuff Boxes, Indian Bells &c."

In the same issue of the above paper, was the following advertisement:

> "CALIFORNIA
>
> Persons going to California should be sure and take some of the celebrated ANTIQUE CHINESE HAIR OIL, that they may possess a beautiful head of Hair on their return. For sale at wholesale and retail at the
>
> China Tea Store
> Price, 37½ cents per bottle.   198 Washington Street"

Optimistic advice to voyagers to the land of opportunity, so that on their return as millionaires, they might look the part!

In the advertising of those days, it will be seen that "California" was the favorite attention-getting headline. It is obvious that there was no Pure Food and Drug legislation in effect, as there were almost daily advertisements by Mrs. E. Kidder, 100 Court Street, Boston, for her medicine which would cure any ills encountered on the long voyage to the gold fields — from Cholera to General Debility and Dyspepsia. She even went so far as to advertise "Sure to cure even where the disease has advanced to the last stage" which seemed to be her slogan or watchword, judging by its repetition in her advertisements.

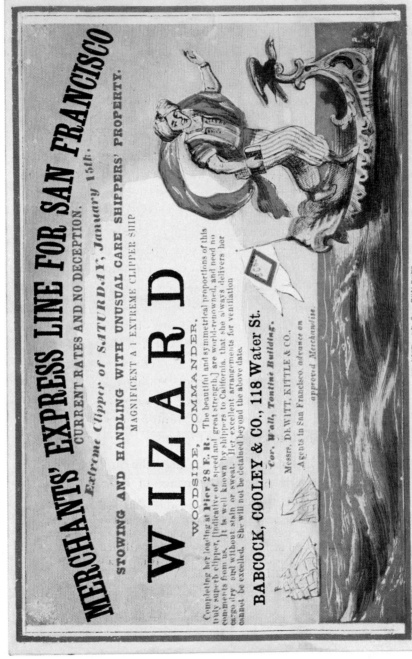

MERCHANTS' EXPRESS LINE FOR SAN FRANCISCO

CURRENT RATES AND NO DECEPTION.

Extreme Clipper of SATURDAY, January 15th.

STOWING AND HANDLING WITH UNUSUAL CARE SHIPPERS' PROPERTY.

MAGNIFICENT A 1 EXTREME CLIPPER SHIP

WIZARD

WOODSIDE, COMMANDER.

Completing her loading at **Pier 28 E. R.** The beautiful and symmetrical proportions of this truly superb clipper, [indicative of speed and great strength,] are world-renowned, and need no comments from us. It is well known by shippers to California, that she always delivers her cargo dry and without stain or sweat. Her excellent arrangements for ventilation cannot be excelled. She will not be detained beyond the above date.

BABCOCK, COOLEY & CO., 118 Water St.

Cor. Wall, Tontine Building.

Messrs. DeWITT, KITTLE & CO.,

Agents in San Francisco. advance on
approved Merchandise.

SACHET AND CO. PRINTERS

Courtesy of Peabody Museum

WIZARD

SAID TO BE the masterpiece of builder Samuel Hall of East Boston, the "Wizard" was the 84th vessel turned out from his yard. When she arrived at New York she was bought by Slade & Co. for $95,000. Her figurehead was an oriental magician with his book of spells under one arm. In the illustration on the accompanying card, the magician, it will be noted, carries the book in his hand. She ran into stormy weather on her maiden trip and, as happened with many clippers, had to put into Rio for repairs. She then continued to San Francisco and from there went to Hong Kong and Whampoa before returning to New York. On her next voyage she went from her home port to San Francisco and from there to Hong Kong and Akyab (India), Hong Kong again and back to the city of the Golden Gate. She once more made the trip from San Francisco to Hong Kong where Captain Slade, her first commander, died and was buried. Captain Woodside, whose name appears on this card, took over command and brought her back to New York via Melbourne and Manila, losing a whole suit of sails as well as her mizzen topgallant mast in a heavy gale. Bad luck followed her, as far as storm damage was concerned, as on the trip advertised on the card we reproduce, she again ran into strong gales which nearly ended her career. Later, while under command of Captain H. G. Dearborn, on a trip from New York to Acapulco, Mexico, with a cargo of coal, she once more met misfortune and had to keep the pumps going continuously for 24 hours without reducing the water which was four feet deep in the hold. Fortunately she was able to make Port Stanley, Falkland Islands, where she anchored and discharged part of her cargo and tried to stop the leaks. The voyage was resumed but the following day she had to put back to the same harbor because she was leaking so badly. There, the rest of her cargo, except enough for ballast, was discharged. By dint of almost constant use of her pumps, she was able to make her way to New York after a voyage of 41 arduous days. After necessary repairs had been made, she was sent to London where she was sold. Renamed "Queen of the Colonies," she made several passages between Liverpool and Australia as a member of the Black Ball Line. She is reported to have ended her rather luck-less career by being wrecked in 1874 en route from Java to Falmouth, England.

Reference to the famous Black Ball Line recalls the following verses from "American Sea Songs and Chanteys" by Frank Shay, published 1948 by W. W. Norton & Co. Inc., New York, N. Y.—

" 'Tis when a Black Baller is clear of the land,
    To my yeo, ho! blow the man down.
Our boatswain then gives us the word of command,
    Oh, give me some time to blow the man down!

'Lay aft,' is the cry, 'to the break of the poop!'
    To my yeo, ho! blow the man down.
'Or I'll help you along with the toe of my boot!'
    Oh, give me some time to blow the man down!

'Tis when a Black Baller comes back to her dock,
    To my yeo, ho! blow the man down!
The lads and the lasses to the pierhead do flock,
    Oh, give me some time to blow the man down!"

VISUAL TELEGRAPHS

From King's Handbook of Boston Harbor

SIGNAL STATION ON TELEGRAPH HILL, HULL, MASS.
1853

BEFORE the development of the telegraph invented by Samuel F. B. Morse, native of Charlestown, Mass., and a graduate of Yale, 1810, various devices were produced for speeding up communications. The early "visual telegraphs" were rather crude affairs but represented a great advance for those early days in expediting maritime information. Naturally, the merchants and ship owners of Boston were vitally interested in any means which might enable them to get advance notice of the arrival of vessels along our coast. The first long distance signal stations in this country were operated from Martha's Vineyard to Boston by Jonathan Grout, Jr., a graduate of Dartmouth in 1787. At one time there were thirteen of them between West Chop and

VIEW OF THE OLD STATE HOUSE. BOSTON. ABOUT A. D. 1850.

From the Collection of the State Street Trust Company

VIEW OF THE OLD STATE HOUSE ABOUT 1850
WHEN HUDSON & SMITH MAINTAINED A "VISUAL TELEGRAPH" STATION THERE,
AS INDICATED BY THE POLES AND SIGNAL FLAGS ON THE TOWER.

Dorchester Heights, whence final messages were picked up at the "telegraph station" at 112 Orange Street, out on the Neck. This "line" was in operation from 1801 to 1807. It is from these old stations along our coast that so many heights of land get the name of "Telegraph Hill."

John R. Parker was perhaps the most successful operator on the Atlantic seaboard. He carried on his service from 1822 until 1844, when he sold his "telegraph" line to two of his employees, Joseph Pope, who had been in charge of the Hull station since 1825, and T. A. S. Brown. They shortly resold to Robert E. Hudson and John T. Smith, who carried on operations as Hudson & Smith until 1852, when the development of the electric telegraph put them out of business. It was during this period that they had their "home office" in the Old State House, Boston. In 1853 Pope operated a magnetic telegraph wire between Hull and Boston, later extended to Highland Light. Pope, therefore, had the distinction of serving at the Hull station under both the semaphoric and electric systems. The station at Hull is shown in the illustration at the head of this story. Other operators of visual telegraphs serving Boston were Samuel Gilbert and his successor, Samuel Topliff, who in 1814 took over and expanded the business established by Gilbert in 1810.

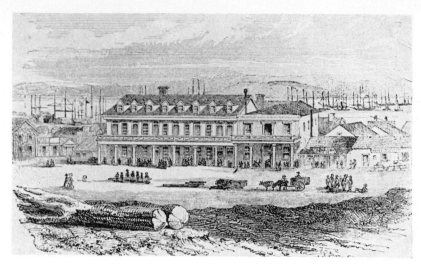

THE PARKER HOUSE OF SAN FRANCISCO 1849
WITH HARBOR IN BACKGROUND

Kindness of The Society of California Pioneers, Albert Frank-Guenther Law, Inc.,
and Paul E. Landry, Assistant to President Glenwood J. Sherrard
of the famed Parker House of Boston.

THIS SAN FRANCISCO PARKER HOUSE, owned by Robert A. Parker of Boston, Massachusetts, and John H. Brown, was erected on the present site of the old City Hall. On the ground floor was a dining room, and a room for billiards, while the second floor was used for gambling, with offices and bedrooms upstairs. The opening of the Hotel was a great event and a California paper thus described the occasion: "The ballroom, the most magnificent and spacious in the country, was graced by the loveliness of many lands. The staid matrons and quiet maidens of our own Atlantic States, the gay daughters of Erin, the gazelle-eyed maidens of Alta, California, mingled with the gay uniforms of the army and navy, shone conspicuously in the brilliantly lighted room." During the summer of 1849 several hundred vessels often lay in the harbor, many of which never sailed again. The population of San Francisco on January 1, 1849 was estimated at only 1,000. The streets at that time were described by one adventurer as almost "jackassable." A much frequented street was a combination of one hundred pound bags of Chilean flour, a long line of cooking stoves, a damaged piano which bridged a gully, ending in a double row of boxes of shoes.

U. S. POSTAGE STAMP
ISSUED IN 1948
COMMEMORATING THE 100TH ANNIVERSARY
OF THE DISCOVERY OF GOLD
IN CALIFORNIA

THE STAMP *which we copied was contributed by Everett R. Cook,*
President of the State Street Trust Company Stamp Club, made
up of members of our staff. The original is purple in color.

CAPTAIN JOHN A. SUTTER, a Swiss army officer, who built the
mill commemorated on this stamp, was born on February 15, 1803
in Switzerland, coming to America in 1834. He first purchased
land in Missouri, but four years later took the Oregon trail to
California, where he was given a grant of 49,000 acres of land on
the Sacramento River by the Mexican Government on condition that he would fortify and develop it into a strong Mexican
outpost. He became a citizen of that country and was given the
title of "Commissioner of Justice and Representative of the
Government on the Frontier of the Rio del Sacramento." He
built a strong fort and several other buildings, including a mill,
tannery, distillery, etc. He acquired more land until his holdings
ran to more than 98,000 acres and developed it into the greatest
trading post in the West. Later, when California became part
of the United States, Sutter decided a new sawmill was warranted because of the increase in population and it was while
John W. Marshall was digging the mill race for the new mill for

him that the famous discovery of gold was made. Though Sutter tried to keep this secret, he was unsuccessful and soon his property was overrun by gold seekers from whom he could not protect himself. This turned out to be the foundation of the development of the present city of Sacramento, now the capital of California, and of the rapid settlement of the whole state. Misfortune seemed to follow Sutter from that time on, as the United States Supreme Court found the title to thousands of acres of his land invalid and he ended up in bankruptcy. From 1871 till the time of his death in Washington, D. C., on June 18, 1880, he petitioned Congress annually for reimbursement without success. Congress had once more adjourned without taking recognition of his claims on the day he died.

It might be appropriate here to include this excerpt from "American Sea Songs and Chanteys From the Days of Iron Men and Wooden Ships" Edited by Frank Shay, Illustrated by Edward A. Wilson, W. W. Norton & Co. Inc. 1948.

> "And it's blow, boys, blow,
> For Californi-o!
> For there's plenty of gold,
> So I've been told,
> On the banks of the Sacramento!"

Historical Collections

MAIN OFFICE

Ship models and old prints in an atmosphere reminiscent
of the early Colonial counting houses, including many
nautical and historical items added during the
past year when our Trust Department moved
into its new rooms on the fourth floor.

UNION TRUST OFFICE

Models, prints, etc., depicting the progress of aviation
from balloon and glider days to the present.

STATE STREET TRUST COMPANY

STATE STREET TRUST COMPANY

BOSTON, MASSACHUSETTS

★

*MAIN OFFICE
Corner State and Congress Streets

★

UNION TRUST OFFICE
24 Federal Street

★

*COPLEY SQUARE OFFICE
581 Boylston Street

★

*MASSACHUSETTS AVENUE OFFICE
Massachusetts Avenue and Boylston Street

★

*Night Depository Service Available

★

Member Federal Reserve System
Member Federal Deposit Insurance Corporation

THE RAND PRESS
BOSTON